ENDORSEMENTS

Ann Coulter has been stealing [Daisy Cutter's] stuff for years.

—"Nickie Goomba,"
Award-Winning Blogger

Daisy Cutter has mellowed a bit ... though I am not the "[Bush] White House Communications Director" as he suggests ...

—Hugh Hewitt,
Nationally-Syndicated Talk Radio Host, Salem Radio Network

Reading Rick Rutledge's Daisy Cutter was a trip down memory lane. He was a good student in my class at The University of Texas and he's a good man who loves his family, his country, and God. We need more like him.

—Marvin Olasky,
Editor-in-Chief, *World Magazine.*

Daisy Cutter

Clearing a Landing Zone for the Deplorables

Rick Rutledge

Marine—Lawyer—Patriot

Daisy Cutter
Clearing a Landing Zone for the Deplorables
Rick Rutledge

ISBN-10: 1727785002
ISBN-13: 978-1727785005

Cover design by MikeLoomis.CO
dcspeaks.net

Contents

Dedication

This book is for Rich DiGiorgis, aka "Nickie Goomba," a great blogger and a better man. Rich lost his battle to cancer in January 2017, and I miss him every day.

This book is also for Rhod, the old soldier who made Daisy Cutter a much better place.

It is also for that Navy vet in Florida who emotionally told me his Vietnam Veteran hat was for those who didn't come back.

And it is for every American who loves this land.

Introduction

"The BLU-82B or 'Daisy Cutter' was the largest conventional bomb in existence (until the MOAB ['Mother of All Bombs']) and is 17 feet long and 5 feet in diameter, about the size of a Volkswagen Beetle but much heavier. … Because of the cumbersome size of the Daisy Cutter and its deadly results, it must be uniquely deployed and detonated. It is launched on a delivery trolley and forced out the back of a C-130 cargo plane. The plane itself must be at least 6,000 feet off the ground to avoid the bomb's massive shock wave. Once clear of the plane, the Daisy Cutter releases its own parachute. …The bomb … inflicts heavy damage, generating pressures in excess of 1,000 pounds per square inch near the point of impact, and the shock waves can be felt miles away."—Urban Dictionary

Long before the Daisy Cutter was deployed against jihadis in Afghanistan, it was used for its original purpose—that is, clearing landing zones for helicopters in Vietnam. I called my blog "Daisy Cutter" because I thought it was appropriate for the times, but also because I thought the name was cool. Okay, mainly I thought the name was cool. Now, it's a throwback, so it's doubly cool.

But this book is here because the content was and remains timely and relevant. And the landing zones being cleared here are of the ideological sort.

I started blogging in the early morning hours of June 28, 2004 with a post entitled "Houston, we have lift off … ." My insight that "rocked" the internet on that first night was as follows:

> Well, here I am. My name is Daisy. Daisy Cutter, that is. Have been wanting to get started, but just could not figure this whole thing out. Started looking at some of them, what do they call them … "blogs" tonight. Lots of crazies out there. Racists, people who want ideological purity at all

costs, people blaming America for people getting
their heads lopped off by crazies in the Middle
East. They're all crazy. If you want the truth, fair
and balanced, you have come to the right place.

From that very humble beginning, I posted another 656 times over the next six-plus years. Eventually, I settled on the pen name, "DC," you know, kind of like the Captain America of Blogging. It fit.

Daisy Cutter was eventually linked/cited by the likes of Glenn Reynolds at *Instapundit*, *Slate*, CBS News, Hugh Hewitt, and the *New York Times*, among others.

Reading and linking great blogs like *Instapundit* and *Ace of Spades* (both of which I still read today) provided insight and inspiration, as did the back-and-forth with bloggers such as Don Surber (author of *Trump the Press* and *Trump the Establishment*) and Dan Riehl, f/k/a "The Carnivorous Conservative" and later of *Breitbart News*. A loyal cadre of readers kept me sharp, as well, as did battles with lefty commenters such as "Pussguzzler" and "Pusillanimous Wanker." They couldn't understand the names we called them without a thesaurus, but hey ... It was their choice to match their knives to our guns. Yes, we had a lot of fun along the way.

I guess it "took a village" to build a Daisy Cutter. Thanks, Secretary Clinton.

For a time, I wanted to keep the blog up on the internet in perpetuity thinking perhaps my kids might read it someday. Ultimately, though, I decided to pull the blog down and keep it in a format that would be accessible for those who may want to read it at some point.

In the process of taking the blog down and putting the posts into an accessible format, though, the idea for this book was born. Namely, as I started grouping the posts into subject matters, I discovered something—my posts over time were telling a story. Actually, they were telling two stories.

First, they were telling *my* story. As you will see, a number of the posts are auto-biographical and stories themselves, describing not only what I believe, but also how I came to believe it and the people who influenced me along the way.

I was also surprised to discover/re-discover that the blog, and now this book, tells the story of my evolution from dedicated Bushie to frustrated Republican to 2016 Ted Cruz supporter to ultimately … a no-account "Deplorable." A lot of the events, themes, and issues that led to the rise of Donald Trump are chronicled here … and 10 years before the fact. While I hardly purport to speak for others who may support the Trump Administration, I suspect that a number of people may recognize and identify with my journey. For those who are not Trump fans, perhaps this book presents an opportunity to understand. But keep in mind: The book is about ideas; any one taking any of this personally is missing the point. It's the ideas, stupid … or something like that.

The chapters are organized by topic as follows:

Chapter One: The Coalition of the Winning: Culture. National Security. Liberty These three tenets form the core political philosophy that runs through the book. Here, this winning philosophy is explained and defended. While I purport to speak for no one but myself in these pages, I do believe that that much of America's conservative movement, and in particular, its more deplorable elements, will find edification and encouragement herein.

Chapter Two: America Began as, and Remains, a Declaration of War—Unlike any other nation in history, America is really a revolutionary and provocative creed for all people and for all time. In this chapter, we exegete our founding texts, thus illuminating the bases for our patriotism. Encouraging our fellow citizens, especially our young people, to understand and appreciate our foundational principles and core values is vital to preserving them and the nation itself.

Chapter Three: Exposing Kerry, The New Soldier, and Winning in 2004—This chapter details my efforts to help re-elect George W. Bush, in particular via a campaign that I ran on John Kerry's infamous but little-known anti-war screed, *The New Soldier.* I, along with many other conservatives, fought hard in 2004 to help re-elect the president. We fight hard for our candidates, and we expect them to do the same for what we believe.

Chapter Four: Taking on Militant Islam—Here, I do the work that the Bush Administration refused to do—namely, casting aside political correctness to take on Islamic terrorism in the arena of ideas. These posts lay out the philosophical case for defending America and the West from extremism.

Chapter Five: Brushed Back by the Establishment—Getting up and Defeating the Harriet Miers Nomination to the Supreme Court—Some of the most nerve-wracking and fun days of Daisy Cutter occurred during the campaign against Pres. Bush's ill-advised Miers nomination to the Court. This brought me face-to-face with the Establishment and its mouthpieces. And we showed we could face them down and win.

Chapter Six: I Fought the Law and the Truth Won—Here, I break down the key legal issues that define the struggle to maintain the rule of law in America, most notably preserving the life and dignity of every individual and eradicating the politicization of the courts.

Chapter Seven: Just a U.S. Marine, but Plenty Enough—Supporting and defending those who are serving today and those upon whose shoulders we stand is vital. In honoring our troops' service to the nation, my hope is this is an exhortation to continue to produce those who will get it done again.

Chapter Eight: The Iraq War—I was Wrong about it Before I was Right About it—The Iraq War was a, perhaps *the*, defining issue of the second Bush term. And like most conservatives, I made the case for it … and forcefully so. As it wore on, however, the war turned into nation-building. But at least there was WMD. Wait …

Chapter Nine: All in All We're Just Another Brick in the Wall—Immigration has been a raging national debate since the mid-2000s. In the summer of 2007, a group of establishmentarians in the Senate tried to sneak through "Comprehensive Immigration Reform," but the lights were turned on by a number of us conservatives and they scampered off into the night instead. A decade later, candidate and later Pres. Trump, gave voice to many Americans' desires to protect the border.

Chapter Ten: Perfect Storm —Sports and Texas Weather—What is this chapter doing here? It is here because it is part of my story and the overall story of both the blog and those who read and loved it (i.e., some of today's Deplorables … or are we "Dregs" now?). And our lives are (thankfully) much more than politics. Plus, as Andrew Breitbart observed, all politics is downstream from culture. Additionally, the most controversial and commented-upon post in the history of Daisy Cutter is in this section—a light-hearted, anti-soccer diatribe. Other significant sporting events are covered, as well, along with our multiple brushes with hurricanes on the Texas Gulf Coast.

Chapter Eleven: Moderation in the Pursuit of Victory is no Virtue —The Awkward Dance that was the McCain Campaign Begets the Obama Debacle—I came out of blogging "retirement" to try to push John McCain past Barack Obama, to no avail. The loss was painfully instructive, and in a lot of ways the last straw for conservatives who now knew beyond question that the Republican Establishment's dalliance with them was a one-sided affair.

Chapter Twelve: Atheists are Scarce in Bomb Craters—Faith is a bedrock value of America, and the Christian faith in particular was critical to the nation's founding. Faith motivated many Trump voters, as well, though a number of Trump critics still wonder why. Perhaps the discussion of faith herein can help explain. If you don't share my faith, we can certainly still be friends. Can those who don't share my faith still be my friend, though? I sure hope so.

Chapter Thirteen: Sgt Pepper's Lonely Hearts Club Band —Enjoying the Show and Getting by with a Little Help from my Friends—The chaos, laughs, and the commenters that made Daisy Cutter go are featured in this final chapter. Here, the fun, the ideas, and the madness all come together to display the heart of the conservative movement that would rather actually do things to preserve the country instead of merely electing Republicans … and … have a little fun along the way.

All told, 102 of the original 657 Daisy Cutter posts are here. Links have been removed, and grammatical/spelling errors in the original posts corrected. In a few locations, I have put explanatory material in brackets. Otherwise, the posts are here as essentially as they appeared on the blog on the dates noted, minus edited portions (denoted by ellipses). The "Note" sections introduced by bold type at the end of posts are my present-day reflections done a la blog comments. The "DC Shutdown" paragraphs at the end of each chapter briefly put the content of the foregoing chapter in current context while introducing the next chapter. Except for the last picture, all the photos in this book actually appeared on the blog.

I hope the posts and columns herein will cause readers to think about the foundational principles that undergird America, because understanding, defending and promoting them is vital to keep America as that "shining city" among nations, or, put another way, to keep America great. I honestly hope, no, I really believe, there is something here that will challenge just about everyone, too. Conversely, I also believe that that there is something here to encourage and inspire just about everyone. It might sound strange coming from someone like myself who is absolutely committed to absolute truth, but … none of us has a corner on it. That is part of being fallible. So, we keep learning and growing.

Still, the bedrock principles that are true remain. You will see that these principles are defended, and with the spirit of a happy warrior, in these pages.

Speaking of warriors, I am donating 25 percent of the proceeds from this book to the Semper Fi Fund (semperfifund.org), a worthy charity that provides urgently-needed resources and support to post-9/11 combat wounded, critically ill and catastrophically injured members of the U.S. armed forces and their families. So, you are already helping to do something good by purchasing this book. And I thank you.

I also especially want to thank the following for helping me turn this project into reality: Brian Allison and Dave Preston provided me with invaluable comments that made this book more readable; what is here (and some of what is not) was greatly impacted by their insightful comments. Kem Oberholtzer also helped me come up with the title. Additionally, Christina Boothe was an early fan of this project, providing encouragement as to how to put this book together and promote my ideas. Finally, thank you to Mike Loomis for understanding my "deplorable" mind, putting together a great cover concept and getting this thing loaded and airborne.

Rick Rutledge ("DC")
October 30, 2018

Chapter One

The Coalition of the Winning:

Culture. National Security. Liberty.

22 July 2004

Coalition is Not Compromise

We are at war, in case you haven't noticed, and thus I have little patience these days for the "perfect church" crowd. Let me explain. You see, I believe in a perfect church. However, it is not located on this side of the Celestial City. Before we pilgrims cross the river to that holy place and meet Jesus Christ face to face, we should be skeptical of claims that any church, which is populated merely by fallible sinners, is perfect. As Dallas Theological Seminary's sage Dr. Howard Hendricks argued years ago, "If you find a perfect church, don't join it. You'll ruin it."

Yet, various well-meaning types, believing earnestly that their doctrine in all areas of life is indeed perfect, still try to impose a standard of perfection upon governmental institutions that is not even sustainable in a church, much less a congressional committee room. The result is disillusionment and ultimately windmill tilting in commune-like, counter-culture movements masquerading as meaningful political involvement. That's a fancy way of saying, they are wasting their time while pretending to do something important. However, for those on the left inclined to vote for Ralph Nader, I say "Go Ralph Go." If the enemies of American security want to cast a de facto vote against Kerry, they have my full support.

My concern is with conservatives, in particular, Christian conservatives —whose natural allegiances should be with Pres. Bush —that toy with either not voting or with voting for Libertarian or Constitution party candidates because of the president's perceived shortcomings. I wish these windmill-tilters were just wasting their time. However, such misguided endeavors can be dangerous, particularly in this time of war, when our national survival is indeed on the table.

Further, these efforts are foolish and counter-productive, because the end result of a Bush loss is a Kerry victory and vice-versa. Thus, the perfect church crowd seeks a cure it admits is worse than the current "disease." ...

The Bush critics on the right might have one of these debates to preserve the union interrupted by a dirty bomb explosion some day if they are successful in ousting Pres. Bush. In 2000, recall that a number of Christians stayed home because of disappointment in revelations that Pres. Bush was driving under the influence many years earlier in Maine. As a result, we all nearly had Al Gore in the White House on 9/11. Was it wise to "stand on principle" because of Pres. Bush's DWI? The jihadis think so.

This past week, I was greatly encouraged when I came across one of the best discussions of the risks of perfect-churchism, in a column written by Dr. Marvin Olasky of *World Magazine*. ...

Dr. Olasky's main point: Coalition is not compromise. It is hanging together, and, as Benjamin Franklin noted, without it, we will "hang separately." Thus, we need all conservatives today to pull together with the only political party that welcomes us and has a chance of winning not only the election, but also the truly life-or-death War on Jihad.

18 January 2006

What exactly is a leftist? A conservative?

I've done a lot of thinking about this subject over the last few years. I have heard various definitions of both leftists and conservatives for some time now, but these haven't seemed workable.

For instance, some define the Left as being "pro-government," but such a definition is shallow and doesn't account for the Left's disdain for certain branches of the government, such as the police and the military. On the right, some have posited (most notably Rush Limbaugh) that "freedom" is the unifying principle for conservatives. This has a certain ring to it, but what do you make of mainstream conservative positions on cultural issues and law and order?

I have been tempted in the past to use the Potter Stewart/porn approach: I know them when I see them. For example, Ted Kennedy … leftist? Check. Ronald Reagan … conservative? Check. Howard Dean … leftist? Check. William F. Buckley … conservative? Check.

But now, I have a definition to pass on to my kids and answer that burning question: "Dad, what is a damleftist?"

So, here's what I think: In simple terms, the more one embraces the post-modern view of mankind, the more he or she is a leftist; the more one embraces a traditional or Judeo-Christian view of mankind, the more he or she is a conservative.

To provide a bit more explanation, the prior definition doesn't rest on one's acceptance of any faith, per se, just the view of mankind as being either post-modern or traditional/Judeo-Christian.

To further break down this definition, the post-modern view of mankind is essentially: The unlimited, unconstrained individual, whose personal reality is defined entirely without resorting to what the philosophers call "metanarratives," i.e., religion, family, country. The individual is supreme in all respects, in making decisions and in defining reality as he or she sees fit.

The traditional/Judeo-Christian view of mankind says that each individual has dignity, yet is limited. The individual does not define the universe, but is part of it.

Whew.

Again, none of us fits perfectly on this philosophical continuum. We all have our "heresies." But I think this is the best way to determine and define who is a leftist and who is a conservative.

So, let's give the definition a test drive.

How about an easy one? Take permissive social mores on sexual issues, for instance. The Left looks to the individual to decide whether a relationship "works" or feels right. The Right generally looks to rules or traditions to decide whether conduct is permissible or healthy.

The free enterprise system? In some ways, this is so antithetical to postmodernism that it considered a "metanarrative." More fundamentally, though, the free enterprise system runs on an understanding of the limits and self-centeredness of individuals. Leftists don't see the need to incentivize the radically unconstrained individual. I mean, would you put God on a rewards system?

It's not always self-evident, though. Why is it that radical individualists seem to gravitate to totalitarianism? If you start from the premise that a Leftist is not required to be consistent (because each individual defines his reality without reference to any external rules or standards), then everything starts to fall into place. Plus, there are other factors, too, such as the following: A totalitarian leftist state works real well for the individuals running it.

Environmentalism? The Leftist view here is primarily a reaction to conservative institutions and the traditional view of mankind itself, namely the view that advocates human dominion over nature.

Back to the Potter Stewart approach ... Is there any doubt that Ted Kennedy is a paradigm of the radically unconstrained individual? ...

9 November 2006

Libertarians are odious and to be scorned, and other lessons from Election '06

... Libertarians and Other Perfect-Church Third Party Types Should be Allowed to Attend Meetings But Should Not be Allowed to Vote—In Montana, reliably conservative Conrad Burns was defeated by the leftist Tester by 3,000 votes. I looked at the vote total and learned that 10,000 blazing idiots provided the margin of victory by voting for the Libertarian candidate. Why? Well, it seems they wanted to be heard. I think I did hear the faint cries from Big Sky on Election Night: ... It appears that the Conservatives on Drugs were upset about the Patriot Act and its

potential limits on their freedom. What?!! It seems that [they] didn't realize that Tester can't and won't do anything about the Patriot Act. But he can hold them upside down and shake every last coin out of their pockets. Maybe some porn and/or pot will fall out, too. But to Tester and the libertarians, that's okay. It's the hypothetical freedom, baby. So, now we get Harry Reid and Co. setting the Senate agenda. Surely, that's better for liberty.

Here's what you need to know about libertarians and their third-party kinfolk and so-called "independent" types of all stripes, you know, those too high and mighty to ever associate with a political party: They believe they are either too virtuous or too smart to work with or for a political party. Truth is, they are neither virtuous nor smart. In fact, they lack common sense and should sit out elections until they get some. In wartime, these perfect-churchers can get Americans killed if they are able to affect elections. Sound harsh? Well, a Demo Senate awaits and we will have no more conservative SC justices for the foreseeable future. You can thank the libertarians in MT for that. Elections are won by gaining majorities and forging coalitions. Finding a half-dozen disgruntled likeminded rejects does not qualify as a coalition. …

Note: To be fair, my ire in the foregoing post is directed at those libertarians who would rather elect a Democrat than an imperfect candidate who shares some but not all of their values. In other words, pragmatic, necessary coalitions "trump," so to speak, "perfect" ideology … including that of the NeverTrumpers of today. There are consequences to seeking perfect candidates in this imperfect world (usually electing Demos, it just so happens). And, as of this writing, John Tester is still lodged like an impacted wisdom tooth in the Senate.

4 December 2006

You know I am a team player …

Still, there's a time to huddle up and address what ails one's team. I have often spoken out against the "perfect church" crowd for trying to solve intra-party and intra-movement squabbles in general elections. Such tactics never fail to benefit the opposition.

So, how did you conservatives like 8 years of Clinton?

The time and place to get things right is among friends (or at least not while mutual enemies are encouraging the scrape). This is what off-years and primaries are for.

Now, you all know that when '08 rolls around that I won't be supporting any Democrats. I didn't fall off a turnip truck. The odds are that I will be there hanging on that G.O.P. lever like I always do. Now, if John McCain manages to bamboozle enough primary voters to get the Republican nod, we'll just have to see, won't we?

But now's the time to get back on track and back to basics, or we could say it's time to get back to the conservative base that made the Republican Party a majority. I am hopeful that we will see such a movement as we go forward. I will remain cautiously optimistic.

In the foregoing spirit, I share with you a phone conversation I had today with a pleasant young man who called me from D.C. on behalf of the G.O.P.. He encountered me in somewhat of a bad state of mind, for sitting in a federal courtroom for most of a morning will do that to you. But still, I wouldn't take any of it back.

So, here's a summary of how it went:

G.O.P.-Man: Good morning, may I speak to Mr. Daisy Cutter?

DC: Yes, this is he.

G.O.P.: Mr. Daisy Cutter, I am calling on behalf of Chairman Ken Mehlman to thank you for your generous support of Pres. Bush and the Republican Party. Also, I wanted to find out if you would be so kind to renew your membership for 2007.

DC: Well, I'm kinda tapped out. Plus, I just gave you guys a bunch of money and renewed in the late part of last year.

G.O.P.: Yes, sir, but that went for our election efforts. Also, your RNC membership runs from December to December.

DC: I see.

G.O.P.: So, can we count on you, as one of Pres. Bush's strongest supporters, to renew your membership at this time?

DC: Well, honestly, I'd rather wait for a bit. Frankly, we just got our heads handed to us because Republicans are afraid to act like Republicans. I want to see how they are going to stand up to the Demos, take for instance on immigration. Also, we need to have the courage to call our enemy by name. I want to see how things go, and then I will decide on what I will do next.

G.O.P.: Sir, I thank you for your candor.

DC: You're welcome.

10 January 2007

I got a confession to make.

I have developed these systems over the years that help me to do things. Decide things. It takes some time to develop them, but they are tried and true.

Light's red. I just stop. No need to question why or breeze on through if no one is around. No need to try and thread the needle just to show off. Stopping at those things is preordained for me. Hot outside? No coat. I mean, I could wear one. But it really isn't necessary. Already tackled this. The system says no coat.

I see a hippie at a "Legalize Medical Marijuana" booth on Venice Beach. No need to check. I already have run the numbers. He is hitting the medicine cabinet. …

Our systems seldom let us down.

Okay, so where is this going?

Well, Ted Kennedy is as reliable a detector of good and evil as there is in Washington, D.C. He really is. I am hard-pressed to find a better weather vane than old Ted.

When he was working with Bush on the Education Bill, it was preordained that there would be dastardly pork, goodies and unwieldy regulations throughout. And his signature on McCain's immigration bill (speaking of indicators, I have a complex formula that involves dividing the Kennedy evil quotient by Pi.), was a sure indicator that the thing was a disaster. He likes John Kerry, etc. It's fool-proof.

And Ted doesn't like the new Bush Iraq plan at all. He is even threatening to cut off funding to the troops (which the Demos will never do). Thus, it must be fairly good. It's at least a dramatic improvement over what we all were fearing with the Iraq Study Group.

Here's another indicator that is as reliable as Ol' Faithful: When Democrats praise the non-partisanship and inclusiveness of Republicans, that means that the Republicans are up to no good.

So, I saw today that Nancy Pelosi and Harry Reid are complaining that Pres. Bush allowed them "no input" into his new Iraq policy. … This is a good sign. Who do they think they are? His spouse? They get no input, unless it is granted. And that would be a mistake. It's always a mistake to do what the Demos want you to do. Always.

Remember when Nancy Pelosi corrected Brit Hume after she was elected Queen of Congress and told him that the objective was not winning in Iraq, but rather "solving a problem." These people don't have a plan for our success in Iraq, and candidly there is no evidence that they want us to win there. And what right do this congresswoman from California and senator from Nevada have to give their input to the commander-in-chief, anyway? None.

And what do either one of them know? Pelosi's claim to fame is being a grandma. Reid is a pretty crafty land dealer. But they have no national security expertise, and they weren't elected to be commander-in-chief. Beat it.

So, based on these tried and true indicators, the troop surge policy, with an eye toward and end-of-year handover to Iraqis, seems to be a step forward rather than backward.

I don't know yet what the president will say regarding the rules of engagement. Here's hoping that our troops are given rules of engagement that free them up to clean up. We will see. And we don't know yet what the plan is with respect to the Shitte militias. Al Maliki may be hedging his bets by keeping friendly with these radical Shiites. Maybe if the surge in Baghdad works, al Maliki will warm to doing what is necessary with respect to Moqtada al Black Teeth. Again, we'll see.

But if Ted says the light is red ... by all means, go.

16 March 2007

The Freak Show Unabated

Emboldened by the Libby verdict and wobbly Republican responses re: firing U.S. attorneys, this Spring finds the Demos in full flower mania and leftist gorging …

A president has the right to fire all of the U.S. attorneys, and then some. It seems, though, that this Administration is stuck in apology mode. No one can or will take credit for any aggressive actions, only passive ones. As a result, they are left looking apologetic when they ought to be taking credit … and taking credit when they ought to be apologetic.

When you are surrounded by political opponents and outright enemies, you need to be bold and let the chips fall where they may. You have to fight, not hug your way out.

Sensing momentum and with elections still a ways off … I see that Henry Waxman has summoned the "operative" Valerie Plame to the Hill, to investigate … in the people's interests, of course. What a complete crock this is. What a joy to have the opportunity to tell them all. But no one seizes the moment.

The horror of starting down Waxman's cavernous nostrils for days should have been enough to tip the '06 elections to the Republicans, but alas …

The freak show continues to pick up steam. Is there no one in Congress who will stand up and call such lunacy what it is? Is there no one who will mock Waxman, chide Democrats as jihadi-sympathizers …

Momentum is a neutral, but if you're parked on an incline, it's not.

Timidity breeds more of the same.

As does courage.

12 May 2006

Peggy Noonan column …

"The Republicans talk about cutting spending,

19

but they increase it —a lot. They stand for
making government smaller, but they keep
making it bigger. They say they're concerned
about our borders, but they're not securing them.
And they seem to think we're slobs for worrying.
Republicans used to be sober and tough about
foreign policy, but now they're sort of romantic
and full of emotionalism. They talk about cutting
taxes, and they have, but the cuts are provisional,
temporary. Beyond that, there's something
creepy about increasing spending so much and
not paying the price right away but instead rolling
it over and on to our kids, and their kids."

5 May 2007

The Republican Party is Still Reagan's Party

More proof that Republicans are smarter than Democrats: Republicans started off their debates at the Reagan Library. It was a shrewd move, and a nice reminder to the R-Team —Remember the last president who was a real conservative and finished strong.

But must we get started so soon on this interminable presidential campaign? I am sick of it already. And I like to follow politics. But I digress ...

I've told you before, and I'll say it again: I like Pres. Bush. He has his flaws, as have been discussed here and elsewhere, ad infinitum. But I think he deserves credit for doing overall a very good job at fighting the war against Militant Islam worldwide in these extremely challenging times. But my fellow Texan is no Reagan.

What made Pres. Reagan unique was a fusion of several things: 1) He became president during a time of great national despondency and insecurity; 2) he attacked this national despondency and insecurity with personal optimism and a commitment to a his core conservative principles; 3) the smarter-than-the-world set loved to deride him, because 4) he held a child-like faith, first in God and then in America.

And the beauty was that the tension between 3) and 4) above made him even more influential. He was dumb as a fox, and his demeanor and simplicity won allies and encouraged friends. Oh, that we had more such "simpletons" in Washington now.

The media and the left knew him as merely The Great Communicator. He was that, but many failed to understand that he was great because of his ability to communicate ideas that were and are powerfully true.

As much as anyone, he halted the nation's 20-year leftward drift. He challenged liberal dogma, with both conviction and humor. There was a goodness about him that belied the liberal caricatures. He helped build back the nation's military. ... [W]hen I signed up in 1989, I was the beneficiary of this work.

He made conservatism mainstream, not just in the country as a whole but even on college campuses. I was on campus in 1984, when he won a majority of the students' votes at The University of Texas, a.k.a., the Berkeley of the South.

He defeated the Soviet Union without firing a shot. Yes, he did it. Others grab credit, but they are posing charlatans. He would never claim credit, but he is clearly more responsible than any other human.

Recall that it was the infinitely wiser, bureaucrat types such as then-National Security Adviser Colin Powell who pleaded with Pres. Reagan to relent in his demand that Mikail Gorbachev "tear down this wall." Against the advice of all of his inner circle ... all of them ... Pres. Reagan pressed ahead and the Berlin Wall is no more.

He was just dumb enough to believe in his principles. And his country. And they didn't fail him.

I love him, still. And I miss him.

Pres. Reagan brought together national security conservatives, cultural conservatives, and economic conservatives. He welcomed them all, and he encouraged them to welcome each other. I like this, as you probably know. In fact, this ... blog is about serving the "Coalition of the Winning: Protecting National Security. Preserving Culture. Promoting Liberty." That's the Reagan legacy. This blog is part of the

Reagan legacy.

Yes, he wasn't perfect, I know. Only Tom Tancredo [California Republican firebrand and immigration Super Hawk] is (humor alert). Indeed, Pres. Reagan wasn't an Elder of the Perfect Church. He was only the best president of the 20th Century.

Many of those who come now and claim to be following in his footsteps so obviously aren't. Take John McCain, for example. Please, do take him ... as in, take him away. Republican politicians like McCain defy the Reagan legacy in their policy proposals and speeches now, but they dare not take him on directly.

For the nation remembers. And Republicans remember. They want another Reagan.

Which is to say ... they want to win.

DC Shutdown: A coalition emphasizing liberty, culture, security then, and now, is the heartbeat of the movement that has shaken America's political establishment to its core. And building coalitions around these three core values as I have advocated here is something entirely different than Blessed Bi-Partisanship, a.k.a., getting along for the sake of getting along. We want to win, and we want to win more than elections. The political philosophy advocated in the foregoing chapter begins with an unabashed love of America, which is the focus of the next chapter.

Chapter Two:

America Began as, and Remains, a Declaration of War

4 July 2004
"Independent" Thoughts

Some thoughts from this American on this Independence Day:

July 4, 1776 was the beginning of America. On that date, the founders pledged in support of American freedom: their lives, their fortunes, and their "sacred honor." They were right to do so, because July 4, 1776 marked the beginning of a long and difficult war with England ...

You can have peace without conflict. You cannot have freedom without conflict ...

In human events, freedom is the exception rather than the rule, in large part because of the prior thought, and also because ...

Although individual human beings yearn to be and are indeed meant to be free because they are created in the image of God, the fallibility of human beings means that remaining free requires constant vigilance ...

Because you can't have freedom without conflict, you need people with courage to defend freedom ...

It's not natural to face conflict courageously, and thus most people in history have not lived in freedom ...

Courage is a moral quality, and thus, we need morality to defend freedom against all enemies foreign and domestic ...

This nation's founders consistently stated and argued that this republic would not survive without guidance and strength provided by the God of the Bible. This reliance on the Providence of God was a consistent and non-controversial belief in America until the 1960s ...

With the passing of President Reagan, we were recently reminded of just how the late, great president inspired this "City on a Hill" to courageously face down Soviet Communism to defend freedom ...

Now, Pres. Bush has told us that he has a "charge to keep," a sacred appointment, if you will, to fulfill his duties as chief executive of these United States, and these duties after 9/11 have been called into sharp focus ...

This president's number one job is to protect America and defend our freedom. Chase the jihadis into every cave, crack and crevice where they may hide and make them play defense rather than plotting attacks against Americans and ...

Make them pay dearly for making the same two mistakes that all of our prior enemies have made: 1) waking us up; and 2) "misunderestimating" us ...

This fight takes courage ...

This fight takes strength and endurance, for it will be long ...

But we know that in the end, as we beat the Nazis and the Communists, we will prevail over these fascist jihadis, for the same reasons we prevailed over previous totalitarians ...

Because God has blessed America and its people, we have become the greatest nation ever ...

But it's not automatic that we stay that way, because ...

You can have peace without conflict. You cannot have freedom without conflict, so ...

God bless America.

4 July 2005

"We hold these truths to be self-evident ...

... that all men are created equal, that they are endowed by their Creator with certain unalienable Rights, that among these are Life, Liberty and the pursuit of Happiness" ...

And with these and the remainder of the brief but eloquent

Declaration of Independence, the United States of America began on July 4, 1776.

But there were no fireworks.

The founders had no government. Limited popular support. No historical precedent for the radical step they had just taken. No chance of avoiding the consequences for their treason against the crown.

But they did have something. They had a war on their hands. Indeed, they had declared war on the world's greatest power.

Seven years later, the Americans miraculously had outlasted the British Army, and the independence declared on July 4, 1776 was won. Many credited Divine Providence for the victory, for it was so spectacular and miraculous as to defy human explanation.

After all, it was greater than any Hollywood script. The founders' triumph was both the political lunar landing and the greatest military upset in history, all rolled into one. The American Revolution sent shock waves through the world that still reverberate in places like Kiev, Beirut, and yes, in Kabul and Baghdad, too. And more waves are on the way.

For now, history has a precedent that human freedom can overcome all odds to establish a home for the free and the brave.

They made the history that the world views with awe. It's hard for those of us who have grown up in this Wonderland called America to recall that America wasn't always a superpower, let alone the world's lone superpower. Indeed, this whole experiment got kicked off by America sticking its finger in the eye of what was then the world's superpower.

The optimism, braggadocio, and confident spirit of America traces its roots to her daring founders. For they had the foresight to realize the value of freedom, and also the guts to fight for it. If you read the case they laid out in the Declaration, they seemed to be arguing that life simply wasn't worth living if it wasn't lived in freedom. Indeed, they spoke of a "necessity" and a "duty" to fight for liberty.

Without the willingness to fight for freedom, they realized, we won't have it. They showed us the way.

The founders paid dearly, too, with their property, their own physical liberty, their families, and even their own lives. But they persevered. They didn't whine, falter, or quit when the inevitable, bloody fight with Britain came.

They knew it would come to this. They knew the tough days ahead would require more than they could give. And they would give their all.

Consider that they finished the Declaration with these words: "And for the support of this Declaration, with a firm reliance on the protection of Divine Providence, we mutually pledge to each other our Lives, our Fortunes and our sacred Honor."

They would need all that they had pledged and relied upon to make it through the difficult days ahead.

We need to remember their examples on this day ... and every day.

4 July 2006

Through Freedom's Eye We See ... a Blue Sky

I can never say it enough.

It makes me so proud that my nation's first words were an utterance of belief, of raw faith, a bold leap into the sky, riding upon and lifted only by the rushing air of the truth upon which they soared.

Surely the founders knew they were taking a bold leap, as they planted their flag on a political and ideological peak never before discovered, much less ascended.

But I wonder if the founders had ever seen an eagle fly.

I wonder if they fully apprehended the power of the rushing wind that would lift them.

"We hold these truths to be self-evident."

Can't you see, man? These things are self-evident. They needed none of the many lawyers in their midst to prove the truth of their bold proclamation.

All men are created equal. They have certain unalienable rights granted to them by God. They have a right to live, to be free, and to pursue happiness. They have a right to hold a government accountable that doesn't abide by these truths.

We Americans believe in these things. As we hold to them, since they are true, we rise as an eagle taking flight. It is natural and the only way to go. It's the only path we know. Up. Out. Over and above. We are free, so we see things that others only dream of. We risk and thus we reap the results of freedom's dare.

As Americans, we look up. We believe.

And the view is beautiful up here.

Belief is an assurance or confidence of what is, by definition, a mystery. Thus, it always dwells with unbelief. That is, some will always remain unconvinced. This is the nature of free will. In fact, without unbelief, we couldn't even know the nature and joy that is believing in what is true.

Freedom's flight remains a perpetual struggle.

Recently, I was reminded of a trip back from a family reunion in my grandad's car during the mid-70s. I was in the front seat, sitting between my granddad and my dad. They were talking about how surely the Japanese would overtake America as the world's economic leader. Thus, I found myself in the awkward position of arguing with these two men who had taught me to believe in America. "Hey, wait a minute, we'll come back, right? We're Americans."

They knew better, too. My granddad had grown up poor. But he opened a meat market, scratched, clawed, and ultimately became very successful. And my dad, he's the one who told me all about America and why and how to believe. He was a salesman, and just a "rag" salesman at that. Still, he did well. In America, even a rag salesman could do well. This was the land of opportunity. This is what these men taught me. Now, I was arguing with them?

Fast forward about ten years ... I was talking with a friend who went to graduate school at Stanford before going to work at Motorola. His patriotism was waning. Maybe it was the influence of the "enlightened unbelief" at Stanford.

He recounted to me how the Japanese were helping themselves to our computer chip designs. They were having trouble keeping up with

America, because in their culture, the risks associated with innovation were too great.

Still, my friend argued, "What's the difference, anyway? What does it matter if the profits go to Japan or the U.S?" I steamed. What does it matter?!

What does it matter if America prospers? What does it matter, if this, the last, best hope of mankind survives?

What does it matter? Ask the charitable organizations and missionaries why it matters. Ask those who aren't free. Ask the many nations who still look here for help, guidance, support, and encouragement.

What does it matter that this nation, whose very essence is an abiding belief in freedom, survives? What does it matter?

It matters. A lot.

Fast forward again to 1991 ... Then, we heard Saddam boast of the coming "Mother of All Battles," boiling oil, tens of thousands of body bags, etc. Some gulped and wondered openly if America's young troops had the mettle of past generations. Would they be up to the task? But I saw them and knew they would be. They knew they would be, too. These young Americans believed and never blinked, and Saddam's threat became a punchline.

And now our latest generation of troops has also answered the questions posed by Militant Islamists: Would young Americans leave their safe and secure lives to defend not only their freedom but also that of their countrymen? Would they kick down the necessary doors to root out the enemies of this nation? Many of us knew all along they would.

It goes on and on. You bet against America at your peril. I know, some will always doubt and want to bet against my country. But do you feel lucky? Do you?

Because you see, I have seen ... I have seen the eagle fly.

So, while tyrants become the cynics' masters, we will press on and up.

For we owe it to those who first showed us how to soar to keep faith in America. And we owe it to our young people to continue to believe in America. They are looking at us, as we look back at our examples.

Please understand that I am not advocating belief simply for the sake of believing. I am not advocating belief upon a fictional magic carpet, for belief is only as strong as its object. Rather, I am advocating keeping faith in this nation and its founding principles.

Just because it flies and appears magical doesn't mean it isn't real.

Because I have seen the eagle fly. ...

4 July 2007

Happy Birthday America: Freedom is Still Beautiful ... and Controversial

This Fourth of July finds America at war. There have been a lot of Independence Days like this, though, in our history.

But this year, we note that around the globe anti-Americanism is high and seems to be on the rise.

Why is this? Some would argue that American foreign policy is to blame.

I have heard from friends who have been both to Europe and the Middle East that the very same argument to defend anti-Americanism is consistently being trotted out —That is, the world "likes Americans, but they just don't like our government."

However, I think this is a cop-out that masks the true feelings of many foreigners expressing anti-American views.

To a certain degree, we understand their point about our government. We Americans don't like our government a lot of the time. Still, we don't care much for burning American flags or the President in effigy, either.

Plus, it's our government.

And unlike much of the world that expresses this disdain for our government, we are our government. We understand that our government is a republic, and we further understand that it doesn't represent us perfectly, or even well, at times. But over time, for better or worse, our government is what we, the American people, want it to be.

Our government is really an extension of us because we are free. We are not as free as perhaps we used to be, and we are certainly not as free as we want to be. But we are free.

And our freedom —freedom to speak, to write, to worship ... or not, to work, to dream, to protest, and to vote, and to do all of the foregoing without fear —this is a call to arms to much of the world.

Thus, what the current rise of anti-Americanism really tells us is that freedom is on the decline in the world.

So, we hear the loud voices of the anti-American tide.

But what irony to have the subjects of Muslim autocrats in Saudi Arabia tell us that "They like Americans, just not their government." They speak of us as if we are subjects, like they are. They speak in this way because they are subjects.

In Russia, reports of American warmongering and profiteering are accepted as gospel. Regardless of the facts or the price of gasoline here, they just know that we went to Iraq to steal the oil. Why? The Russian people are ruled by a government that engages in this very thing in spades.

Throughout Europe, the naysaying nieces and nephews of the nanny state wring their hands and deride America for daring to confront the fascists of the 21st century. America's freedom and fight endangers the peace, it seems.

Meanwhile, militant Muslims and their allies worldwide decry the debauchery, excesses and corruption of American society. Yes, freedom produces excesses. But these excesses pale in comparison to societies that are led around by the nose by the likes of Zarqawi, Hussein, Assad, Ahmadinejad, and Bin Laden.

Indeed, tyrants and their subjects never have and never will understand freedom.

Both tyranny and freedom expand and threaten the other's oxygen supply. They war with each other. They must. Always.

America's birth certificate was thus a declaration of war, not just on King George's England but on tyrants in perpetuity.

Therefore, America remains a magnet for criticism worldwide principally because America remains a reminder to the world that a people still dares to live in freedom.

Friends take solace. Foes take heed.

We are America the Controversial, because we are free. We are America the Beautiful.

A few thoughts about American Exceptionalism

… I was inspired … to comment on the phrase that both offends and repels hard-core liberals everywhere: American Exceptionalism.

I feel about that phrase how Patton felt about combat: I do love it so.

I stirred up our ol' pal, Charlie [the liberal blogger at "Pusillanimous Wanker" … yes, that was the real name of his blog], by invoking the phrase in the global warming debate below (we have sometimes strayed into religion around here, you know).

In our debate below, I mentioned that one of the Left's reasons for promoting Environmentalism is that the Left resents American Exceptionalism. Our prosperity is part of that exceptionalism. Thus, the Left resents our big cars, big houses, and the air conditioners that cool them.

In the [prior] thread …, Charlie commented, "We're all people. Daisy, and I am not kidding here... I literally have tears in my eyes... we are all people. Think about that when you want to flaunt "American Exceptionalism" as a virtue. They (whoever "they" are at the time) are people, too. I wouldn't ask you to sympathize with a Palestinian suicide bomber any more than I would ask you to forgive Timothy McVeigh. But the world is filled with people."

I wouldn't express those thoughts in the way that Charlie does, but I agree with his sentiments. That is, I believe, even though I argue and fight hard for what I believe in, that God is bigger than me. His ways are not my ways. I try to keep my fight is on the level of ideas. Indeed, all people have equal value. Actually, I would go farther than Charlie. I think all people (even the really bad ones like Larry Craig [Google "Idaho senator with 'wide stance']) have equal value in God's eyes.

But here is my point: All countries and systems of government do not have equal value. Some are better than others. Others are far, far better than others. America has been, and remains, exceptional among nations.

And by the way … Why is it considered "moving to the center" by Obama when he runs an ad claiming that he loves America? This tells you most of what you need to know about the modern American Left.

Now, listen to what happened while I was responding to Charlie's comment …

I am typing away a response to Charlie, and then …

Our Spanish-speaking cleaning lady comes by my office at about 9:30 P.M. CST. She speaks very little English. By some twist of fate (I think Providence, really), I was watching the Astros. That's not a big deal. It's actually to be expected, because I am a glutton for punishment. But something is wrong with my TV, and this is where Providence meets beliefs … meets real life. The Astros for some reason are in Spanish on my TV this night. Something happened. I think I hit a button or something, and I can't get it fixed. It's only on this channel, too. I still can speak some Spanish, so I am watching and listening. I mean, I can tell what is happening by watching. Plus, I can understand some of what the announcers are saying.

Our cleaning lady comes in my office, hears the Spanish on TV, and asks me (in Spanish) if I speak Spanish. I tell her, "Un poco." She laughs. Then, we have about a ten-minute conversation re: my Spanish-speaking history, including my dad's fluency in the language. I have talked to her before, but never to this extent. She asks me if we have any other lawyers who speak Spanish. I laugh. I have been promoted to Spanish-speaking lawyer. Eventually, I find out that she wants to locate an immigration lawyer for her husband.

So, I am going to find an immigration lawyer for her, and then call her this week and give her a name. I can't speak for what the immigration lawyer will do, but she won't get charged for my time.

The foregoing is a simple, small act that gives insight into what one person believes about the value of other people.

Why do I tell you this? Well, Charlie, et al., it's certainly not to impress those of you who don't know me. Those who do know me well don't seem really impressed by this … blog, so … you can get some insight into what my beliefs really are.

But remember (and I do understand the irony of this point): You won't find out what people really believe on a blog. You can only see it in how they live their lives. Real belief is found in real life. …

Yes, people are the same everywhere. There are great people everywhere, except maybe Arkansas.

But seriously … there are great people everywhere.

But the greatest country is right here. We live in it, by God's grace. I view it as my duty to do my part to ensure that it stays exceptional for future generations.

4 July 2009

Happy Independence Day, America: We are not a government

… The title of this post is as appropriate today as ever, it seems. We've talked about it here before, and a lot. …

But here it goes: America is not a government. America is a nation. A nation has a government. A nation is not its government.

That some don't understand this, like they don't understand gravity when they fling themselves from buildings, is of no moment.

The American nation is fundamentally defined by those of us who share the American ideal at the core of our culture —that all men are endowed by their Creator with certain inalienable rights. Add to that a border and a government, and there is your American nation.

Too many have forgotten this and think that America is all that happens in Washington, D.C. What a small view of the nation. What a small view of life.

I am an American. My dad taught me to be proud of this fact and walk tall. Think big. Whining is not the American way. But winning is.

The current goings-on in D.C. challenge our spirit [the effort to ram Obamacare through Congress on a party-line vote was well underway], but our spirit should never be defeated. Rather, our spirit cannot be defeated. …

DC Shutdown: There are those today who argue that America is not great. There are others who claim that America was always a great nation, but they seem reluctant to make the case. And then there are those who believe that America, not without flaws, has still always been a great nation; even so, it has gotten away from the principles of liberty that made it great. This last group is the one I (and most Deplorables) belong to. And fighting for what we believe—and the candidates we believe in—is what we expect. In the next chapter, I examine how I and my fellow bloggers fought hard to help ensure George W. Bush's second term in 2004, even though the president often seemed unwilling to fight hard for himself.

Chapter Three:

Exposing Kerry, "*The New Soldier*," and Winning in 2004

23 August 2004
Killer Ambush 30 Years in the Making

… The Swift Boat Veterans for Truth. Now, I must tell you, I generally start squids [a "term of endearment" that Marines use for members of our Navy] with two strikes in the count, but these guys are alright. Check 'em out at www.swiftvets.com. They have real mettle, unlike Kerry (whom the SBVT says never got any metal in him bigger than a rose thorn). Make no mistake about it. The SBVT have planned and are executing a devastating ambush on an unsuspecting and arrogant victim. This ambush has been 30 years in the making, and apparently is the product of the group's deep-seated and justifiable anger at Kerry for working the system to get his butt out of Vietnam as fast as possible so that he could return to the States and trash his former comrades. Now it is payback. …

The president today understandably distanced himself (again) from the SBVT devastating ads. However, SBVT's John O'Neill, the co-author of Unfit for Command and Kerry antagonist since 1971 was undeterred while appearing on Rush's radio show. He simply said, "The president is entitled to his opinion." In the same appearance, O'Neill continued to blast away at Kerry: "He is no war hero."

Indeed, Kerry is apparently not a hero. That fact, however, certainly would not and should not disqualify him from being commander-in-chief. However, lying about his record, faking injuries and getting purple hearts for thorn wounds ... this stuff does cause problems. And ... getting an early out so you can come home and attack your "friends" who are still in harm's way, citing Communist propaganda and emboldening the enemy in the process, yes, that disqualifies one from being president. But hey, I'm just a rich Republican operative ... and from Texas.

At the end of the day, this appears to be the punch line for Kerry: He used his military service and attendant credibility to gain political popularity and notoriety upon returning from the Vietnam War, calling American servicemen "war criminals" to stoke the anti-war fires. Now, however, he seeks to claim that his service in that "illegal" war was noble and again wants to use his service and attendant credibility for political gain, i.e., elect me because I served in Vietnam. I have been shot at (debatable, we now learn) and am a war hero, unlike that Chicken Hawk Bush.

The SBVT will hear none of it. They have been betrayed and used before. They are not going to sit quietly by and watch it happen this time. Well, they may wait quietly while Kerry and the dunderheads running his campaign walk up on the next killer ad.

Anchors Aweigh ...

19 September 2004

Just When You Thought It Might Be Safe to Market Yourself as a War Hero

With the Iraq War looking like tough sledding again, Sen. Kerry is predictably testing the political waters. Reports today indicate that he is apparently going to challenge (again) America's mission while her troops are in harm's way ... thus endangering both the troops and the mission.

However, the time for debating the mission is over. Rather, the debate now should be: How do we best accomplish the most decisive American victory? Instead, Sen. Kerry continually seeks to appease the Deaniacs and Michael Moore fringe (aka mainstream Democrats) by recklessly attacking our efforts against the jihadis.

This is a familiar pattern for Sen. Kerry. The Swift Boat Veterans for Truth have now turned to Kerry's troubling anti-war activities while Americans were in harm's way, and for good reason. The SBVT's latest devastating broadside hits Kerry for his flip-flopping about his pitching of his medals. As usual, the most devastating opponent of Kerry is ... er .... Kerry.

If the junior senator from Massachusetts still wants to play the war hero, he's got to answer not only for his questionable four-month service record, but also for how he endangered American troops and the nation's mission against the North Vietnamese Communists after he came back. His anti-war activities ... done while a naval officer ... did just this.

Don't believe me? Ask the Communists themselves:

In the photo [to the left], Sen. John Kerry smiles as he is warmly greeted by Comrade Du Muoi, North Vietnamese Communist General Secretary in … 1993. This photo hangs in the "War Crimes Museum" in Ho Chi Minh City (f/k/a Saigon). The photo is located in a section of the museum dedicated to anti-war protesters. No Kidding.

Kerry's supporters can crow about his service and medals, but let's face the following fact: The last time America faced an expansionist enemy bent upon our destruction, Kerry also ended up as a hero for the enemy.

Kerry still hasn't changed his ways and atoned for his Vietnam transgressions. As such, we can't have confidence that he would not become the jihadis war hero, as well.

Here's the deal: An American war hero, even a legitimate one, may be qualified to be president. An enemy war hero is disqualified. Period. End of story.

25 September 2004

Why this Election Will Not Be Close, Part II

Here's Kerry's magnum opus of his service to the nation during the Vietnam War ... the cover of the book that his campaign has tried to hide. The thing is not in print anywhere ... Note how the hippies on the cover stand in a pose mocking the Marines who raised the flag on Iwo Jima.

The New Soldier was a hallmark of Kerry's efforts to undermine the American effort to defeat the Communists in Vietnam. Kerry was full-fledged into this effort while Americans were fighting and dying in Southeast Asia. This is what was and is in the soul of John Kerry. For those of you on the Left who doubt that such feelings still reside in John Kerry, then when has he apologized for this outrageous, anti-American conduct? When will he apologize?

The answer to this question is found in the new Iraq focus by Kerry. It all sounds eerily similar: Run down the U.S. war effort and embolden the enemy, all the while trying to improve your political standing. This time, the stakes are higher, however. And this time, the country has the experience of Vietnam to avoid making the same mistakes again.

Watch for the SBVT [Swift Boat Veterans for Truth] to lower the boom and hammer this point home in October. God bless 'em. For squids, they're not bad.

Semper Fidelis ...

30 September 2004
Kerry's Book Part 1

Last night on "Hannity & Colmes," author and Kerry buddy George Butler appeared to plug his book: John Kerry: A Portrait. Sean Hannity … held up an actual bound copy of *The New Soldier*, Kerry's 1971 book (that Butler edited) and that the Democrat presidential candidate doesn't want America to see. So, Butler's attempt to capitalize on his buddy's presidential run ironically provided an opening …

And there it was, with the inflammatory and disrespectful cover in full view. I discussed it here three days ago, and displayed the cover mocking the U.S. Marines raising the American flag on Iwo Jima.

Kerry operatives, like Butler, will now have to try to explain away Kerry's effort at undermining the American war effort, while disrespecting and endangering young Americans in harm's way.

Yet, Kerry's words of contempt for America's armed forces are unmistakable. This passage caught my eye:

"The Marines say they never leave behind their wounded. These men have left all the casualties and retreated behind a pious shield of public rectitude. They have left the real stuff of their reputations bleaching behind them in the sun."

Hannity remarked that "this book might become an issue in this campaign." We'll see. If it does, it will probably be up to the pajamahadeen in the blogosphere. …

29 September 2004
Kerry's Banned Book, Part 2

I began my now-until-Election Day analysis of *The New Soldier* by John Kerry … yesterday. I should explain how the book is structured, so you might follow along better. … Every voter should read this book, which has never been renounced by Kerry. He knows it is radioactive, and that explains why his supporters have bought up virtually all of the available copies of it.

The book is divided into six (6) parts: 1) Preface by the editors; 2) Introduction by Kerry, which is a summary of his April 22, 1971 congressional testimony; 3) Chronology of "Operation Dewey Canyon III," the VVAW [Vietnam Vets Against the War] 1971 march on D.C.; 4) Testimonials of supposed veterans and family members about the evils of the Vietnam War and the American troops that fought it; 5) Epilogue by Kerry; 6) Appendix containing a) profiles of the protesters, and b) complete congressional testimony of Kerry.

I will be quoting from various parts of the book, in no particular order. Make no mistake about this book. It is anti-American to the core. Further, it is anti-American during a time when we Americans should have been standing by our troops in harm's way. It seems to strike a familiar theme.

Here's today's quote, from Kerry's Introduction:

"... [I]f you read carefully the President's last speech to the people of this country, you can see that he says, and says clearly, 'but the issue, gentlemen, this issue is fighting terrorism, and the question is whether or not we will leave that country to the terrorists or whether or not we will try to give it hope to be a free people.' But the point is that they are not a free people now, and we cannot fight terrorism all over the world. I think we should have learned that lesson by now."

Pretty incredible, huh? Except Kerry actually said "communism" where I have inserted "terrorism."

It's today that he's making the argument in the quote above.

30 September 2004
Kerry's Banned Book, Part 3

[John Kerry, in *The New Soldier*.] "We are here in Washington to say that the problem with this war is not just a question of war and diplomacy. It is part and parcel of everything we are trying to communicate to people in this country —the question of racism, which is rampant in the military ... the hypocrisy in our taking umbrage in the Geneva Conventions and taking that as justification of this war when we are more guilty than any other body for violations of those Geneva Conventions; in the use of free fire zones, harassment interdiction fire, search-and-destroy missions, the bombings, the torture of prisoners, the killing of prisoners, all accepted policy by many units in South Vietnam."

Questions for the debate (which won't get asked) for Sen. Kerry:

1) Do you still believe that the U.S. military is racist? If not, when did it change, and what changed it?

2) Was the U.S. military guiltier of violating the Geneva Conventions than the North Vietnamese Army ... the Khmer Rouge in Cambodia?

3) Did you endanger U.S. POWs by making the above statement in 1971 while many Americans were held by the North Vietnamese?

4) Should an American denigrate the conduct of his military and its mission during a time of war?

8 November 2004

What it all means: The Cutter Coalition Rules

Well, just about everyone has chimed in by now on what the President's re-election means. I must say, I have got to stop reading the Demo self-flagellation pieces. I am enjoying them too much. As each day passes, they add more venom. It seemingly takes very little time for things to return to normal.

And let me say a word to the conservatives that want to help the Democrats by telling them to go to the center and stop being Leftist madmen: Stop. You are wasting your time. Let them go. They are going to go there anyway. Evan Bayh, Bill Richardson, and Joe Lieberman have proven that they don't have chance nationally with the Demos. Centrist Demos are out of the mainstream. Accept this fact. ...

The Winning Coalition: Security, Culture, Liberty

The Republicans have become a majority party by emphasizing the above three themes. In this election, security and culture were paramount, while liberty (primarily due to increased spending by the Bush Administration) took a secondary role. As long as Republicans can keep the security, culture, and liberty wings happy and involved, the Demos' numbers will continue to shrink. As long as security is at the forefront, Demos are especially in trouble.

A quick word about culture: I am a cultural conservative. However, this election to me was first and foremost about national security. Without security, our culture debates can quickly become theoretical. …

DC Shutdown: Kerry's ill-fated efforts to humanize himself and normalize his candidacy ultimately failed. As predicted, the election was not close, principally due to the conservative base of the Republican Party showing up and working hard for Pres. Bush. The key issues centered around national security; to be sure, the Bush Administration had taken on Islamic extremists operationally. However, seemingly held captive to political correctness, the Administration's efforts to take on the Islamists in the information war were consistently frustrating. In the next chapter, the necessity of engaging in the battle of ideas is examined.

Chapter Four

Taking on Militant Islam

11 September 2006

You might not remember this intersection, but I do.

… It's got a traffic light, and it's in a nice part of suburban Houston.

It's a pretty place, nestled in the towering pines and oaks. It's right around the corner from where I used to live.

I'll never forget it. I was sitting here at the light, waiting to turn right when I clicked on the radio to see what was happening five years ago … today.

ABC was still trying to piece it together. A plane had hit the World Trade Center. It looked as if it could be terrorism, but who knew at this point.

I recall one reporter remarking how this would be a "test" of the new President. Politics, always a political angle with these people, I thought.

Over the course of the day, politics faded, though. And other things started to come into view.

The events of five years ago changed many things. For me, it took some time for the full impact of what had happened to make a new landing zone in my conscience.

But I was changed. This was not insignificant, for my view of the world had been well-settled for many years. So, what happened? This social and economic conservative became a national security-first conservative. This is not to say that my prior views were changed, but circumstances dictated a change of emphasis.

I made new friends ... people like Ed Koch, Phil Hendrie, Zell Miller, and Joe Lieberman. They made new friends, too.

Ultimately, the events of 9/11 stoked a fire in me that became this blog. With my days in the military behind me, I now do my little part here to defend America and her friends ... protecting national security, preserving culture, promoting liberty.

Today, I hope we remember how the tragedy and sadness of 9/11 led to the unity and resolve that we saw at the service in the National Cathedral ... Pres. Bush with the bullhorn ... Congress spontaneously singing God Bless America ... and the lightning-quick response in Afghanistan.

Once again, for a time, politics ended at the water's edge. It was wonderful to behold. And our enemies quaked as the sleeping giant awakened.

But will we forget? Rather, have we forgotten? Have we forgotten the Americans falling to their deaths from the WTC rather than being burned alive? Have we forgotten the maniacal jihadis who would kill us all in the name of Allah? Have we forgotten that our chief offense in the eyes of this enemy is our insistence upon living in freedom?

Some may have forgotten.

But as I remember where I was when I heard the news, I will never forget.

Indeed, I will remember. And I'm teaching my sons and daughters to remember, too. And I'll tell everyone who stops by here to remember ... to love this country and those who defend it ... to do their part, however small ... to never forget ... and to never, never, never give in.

We look back today. And we look forward to victory tomorrow.

24 May 2005

If flushing a Koran would save a life, would you do it?

... I realize my question could have been broader. Indeed, I could have asked: Would you deface or destroy a Bible to save another human being? ...

The crux of the matter here is this: We are weighing two competing values —the value of respecting a book believed to be holy by millions of people (in my question, the Koran) versus the value of saving a human life (in my example, an American life).

To the extent the Koran were to represent God's revelation, in my view, it would be the words and truth communicated rather than the paper and ink they are written on that have true value. Likewise, in my view, the Bible has lasting value because of what it says —not because of the paper and ink that makes up any particular copy.

Interestingly, we have learned recently that some Muslims apparently regard the Koran itself as something worthy of worship. This is a foreign concept to the Judeo-Christian mind, where God alone is worthy of worship. To the Jew and the Christian, the Bible is God's revelation; it is not God.

So, for me, it is not hard to decide that I lean toward protecting human life over the respect for a religious symbol. To the extent that the Muslim world doesn't understand this, my retort is I likewise don't understand their point of view. Just how can people riot and kill other people made in the image of God because of the purported disrespect shown to a copy of the Koran? I realize that certainly a minority of Muslims participated in such an outrage, but where is the Muslim outrage at their conduct? Let's hope that this is just a public relations problem.

This may surprise some of you, but to me, the answer is the same no matter the scriptures involved or the person to be saved. The answer to the question, for me, is simple: Yes. I would do what it took to save the human life —even putting the scriptures in a toilet. But I wouldn't call in *Newsweek* to watch.

Let me explain "why" and provide a bit of background. First, I should say that I have no respect at all for the views of those jihadis who argue that the Koran advocates Holy War and all manner of terrorism against "infidels." To the extent that they seek to destroy the West, we should seek each of them out and do the same. There is no dialogue with such people. Also, to the extent that the Koran itself advocates 9/11-type violence, it also is not worthy of respect, either. Yet, having said the foregoing, I do believe that the sensibilities of the majority of Muslims who do not advocate or support Holy War should be respected.

For me, though, the *Newsweek* incident and the resulting fallout takes me back to more fundamental questions about Islam and how we should respond to it in light of the answers to those questions. Some don't wish to consider these questions, but they are screaming to be asked ... and answered.

For instance, just how many Muslims do believe in Holy War? And does the Koran sanction it? Who is right about whether the Koran sanctions Holy War, anyway? Am I the only person struck with the alleged usage of a religious symbol to supposedly prick the conscience of a terrorist?

Indeed, there is a debate among Muslims (albeit strangely a quiet one) about the answers to these very questions. That is, what does the Koran truly say? Who is truly following Allah —the moderates or the jihadis? Here is how Robert Spencer of jihadwatch.org describes the Islamic concept of "jihad:"

> Jihad is a central duty of every Muslim. Modern Muslim theologians have spoken of many things as jihads: defending the faith from critics, supporting its growth and defense financially, even migrating to non-Muslim lands for the purpose of spreading Islam. But violent jihad is a constant of Islamic history. Many passages of the Qur'an and sayings of the Prophet Muhammad are used by jihad warriors today to justify their actions and gain new recruits. No major Muslim group has ever repudiated the doctrines of armed jihad. The theology of jihad, which denies unbelievers equality of human rights and dignity, is available today for anyone with the will and means to bring it to life.

Spencer presents a sobering picture indeed. Yet, for me, my Christian worldview leads me to two seemingly contradictory conclusions regarding respecting the beliefs of Muslims.

First, I think Islam —even peaceful Islam —is wrong about many things. Fundamentally from my perspective, it is wrong about Jesus Christ. Islam teaches that Christ, like Mohammed, was a prophet. However, Christ taught that He was the Messiah, and that eternal life is found only through faith in Him. In other words, He was not a mere prophet; He was and is God in human flesh. Thus, Islam is self-contradictory. That is, Christ the "prophet" fatally undermined the teachings of the Koran in teaching a completely different way to heaven than Mohammed taught. Ah, details ...

Second, however, I believe that the sensibilities of peaceful Muslims, along with their right to believe what they wish about God, should be respected. Regardless of a person's views about God, Christ taught that each individual must be respected and allowed to make his or her own decisions in matters of faith. Witness the deference shown by the Apostle Paul to the Athenians in Acts 17, all the while making his case for Christ. As Pres. Bush eloquently said in his 2000 speech when he accepted the Republican nomination, "I am tolerant not in spite of my faith, but because of it."

6 February 2006

Muslims continue to rage over cartoons that first appeared in a Danish newspaper

So what will Europeans do now? Will they now retreat into even more militant secularism? Europe has told itself for many years that all religions are equal. Equally false. Equally harmful. Now that the hypothesis is being tested again, I wonder if there is enough of an intellectually honest remnant in Europe to admit what the world now knows: Militant Islam is the world's greatest security threat.

Europe now needs to summon moral courage to face down the totalitarians in their midst. But ironically Europe is finding, and will continue to find, that a culture which is hostile to authentic religious faith has a hard time summoning the courage it needs to face down evil. The Christians and Jews needed to stand up to evil are sadly no longer welcome in large parts of Europe.

Indeed, while sneering at the culture, faith and institutions of the West, the secularists in Europe have cozied up to the serpent that is Militant Islam. Meanwhile, the serpent has grown and is now constricting the very society that has fed and encouraged it. It is a brutal, sad sight.

I marvel. I absolutely marvel at what we are dealing with in Militant Islam. By comparison to what Jews and Christians have had to endure, the very slight affronts that Muslims complain about are comical. Can you imagine an Islamic version of "Piss Christ"?

God forbid ... a holocaust?

Arguing about the propriety of the cartoons misses that point, I think. Muslims contend that Mohammed, an historical figure, cannot even be depicted in pictures. But Mohammed is purportedly a prophet; he is not God. Unbelievable.

The brutal and thin-skinned Islamic response to the cartoon controversy demonstrates again to those who are paying attention that Islam and democratic freedoms are strange bedfellows. It makes one wonder: Can the merits of Islam withstand the scrutiny of the free exchange of ideas? And by the way, has it ever?

Indeed, Islam has throughout history been spread and maintained through force. This is a fact.

It needs totalitarianism to control the flow of information and "insults." This is an opinion, but I think it is demonstrably true.

This is hardly to say that all Muslims are bad people. But their theology is wrong. And the peaceful Muslims are too often silent. Maybe they are afraid. Maybe they are silently trying to reform Islam.

Maybe there aren't that many of them. Who knows? We just don't hear much in the way internal criticism or honest assessments by Muslims of the problems evident within Islam. ...

The militants claim they are the true Muslims. ...

All I know is that I see from Militant Islam the following: institutionalized anti-Semitism, monumental ignorance, paranoid fear of democratic freedoms, brutal oppression of women, and sectarian warfare typical of the Middle Ages.

Yet, some well-meaning types side with the Muslims in the cartoon controversy, arguing that we should avoid "offending their sensitivities." The *LA Times* reported over the weekend that the Vatican said that freedom of expression "cannot entail the right to offend the sentiment of believers."

Wow. What a dangerous and naive statement. My view: If the "believers" are insane and trying to exert world domination, then the sane had better do more than merely "offend their sentiments."

People endowed by their Creator with certain unalienable rights, namely to freely discuss and debate matters of faith. No faith is exempt. Not yours. Not mine.

God is big enough. ...

6 March 2006

But will the Left push a brick wall over on their Man in a Dress?

By now, most of you in the know have heard of the Yale Taliban. It seems the lad, 27-year-old Rahmatullah Hashemi, is wowing his leftist friends at Yale. Just a few years ago, he was an official Taliban representative (deputy foreign secretary) and spokesman. In his Taliban capacity, Hashemi extolled the virtues of woman-hating and gay-bashing.

Now liberalized, Hashemi opines that maybe, just maybe, women should be allowed to vote after all. I mean, this is 20th-century stuff here. And you know, when a jihadi fast-forwards more than a millennium, the lefties swoon. ...

Never mind the fact that Hashemi advocated/approved of anti-Semitism, honor killings, genital mutilation and acid punishment for wayward women ... and crushing homosexuals with brick walls. Leftists still swoon over this unbathed swine.

Why? He hates America. And make no mistake: The Hard Left hates America. Plus, unlike most of these cowards, their boy Hashemi has the guts to do something about it. Heck, he did.

"Get over here, you big hunk of man in a dress." Swoon ... It's a steamy kiss and a revival meeting all in one. The Ivy League has found religion!!

In this sordid episode at Yale, we see again the neat ideological marriage between radically unconstrained, post-modern leftists and Militant Islam. Further, Yale's admission of a former Taliban official displays to all who would but look that the Ivy League Establishment/Left/same thing could care less about its various interest groups, i.e., feminists and gays. These interest groups are only tools to be used to bring down the real enemies —America and the West. The Hard Left's goals are the same as Militant Islam's: Destabilize the social structure to defeat the Great Satan.

Still, an ironic question in all of this is: How long do you think the jihadis would put up with the Left's idea of sexual mores and women's rights if they took power? Long enough to slit the throats of all the leftists who advocated such burka burning. ...

21 June 2006

MSM Cut U.S. Slack for Killing Civilians in Zarqawi Strike

You know, *Time* magazine has been rushing to the head of the line to accuse U.S. Marines of a civilian "massacre" in Haditha. So, I was wondering last week about the questions that might be coming when it was learned that a woman and child exited the earth with Zarqawi.

But apparently the MSM is willing to let bygones be bygones and forgive the U.S. military for killing a 16-year-old girl and an 18-month-old baby boy in the June 8 airstrike.

I am sure you noticed that there was hardly a peep about this. And why?

Because the 16-year-old girl was Zarqawi's wife of three, yes three, years and the 18-month-old boy was Zarqawi's son by his child bride. ...

Why are we not told such things by *Time* and their ilk? And when the MSM does mention them, why are they mentioned in passing, or outright buried?

Perhaps *Time* worries that its readers might be less-inclined to view the jihadis as "freedom fighters" or "minutemen" if more people knew who we were dealing with?

Why doesn't *Time* and the rest of the MSM just be honest and tell its readers that the Zarqawis, bin Ladens, and the rest of the jihadis of the world are just trying to emulate Mohammed? This is, in fact, what the jihadis claim. Why not investigate and let people decide?

We need to understand the enemy. Does the MSM not understand this? I think they do, but for some reason (maybe they can explain), they don't give us the information necessary to "connect the dots," so to speak, to understand and accordingly prepare for the moves of our Militant Islamist enemies.

Like I said, the jihadis' claimed philosophy is pretty simple: Imitate Mohammed. For example, Mohammed killed infidels and sought to establish Islamic law by force. Modern-day jihadis kill infidels and seek to establish Islamic law by force. Mohammed liked to behead infidels. Modern-day jihadis, too. Mohammed had a child bride. Zarqawi, too. Etc., etc.

Robert Spencer of Jihad Watch ties all this together:

> So, to clarify: I am not in the least interested in discrediting Muhammad and Islam as an end in itself. Nor do I think that such a discrediting would be of much use in anti-terror efforts. The importance of critical examination of Muhammad and Islam comes from the fact that jihad terrorists around the world —from Osama bin Laden to Omar Bakri in England and Abu Bakar Bashir in Indonesia and everywhere in between —invoke Muhammad and Islam to explain their goals and justify their actions, as well as to win recruits among Muslims. When

they do that, it becomes important for non-Muslims, and in particular those in government and law enforcement positions, to know how they do it, so that such efforts to invigorate and expand the jihadist ranks can be effectively countered. In that case, a refusal to acknowledge these unpleasant elements of Islam becomes a hindrance to anti-terror and human rights efforts.

To wit: I would never have thought it a matter of importance to non-Muslims that Muhammad took a 9-year-old bride at the age of 52 (see Sahih Bukhari, vol. 5, bk. 58, no. 236) were it not for the fact that child marriage is rampant in the Islamic world, and that that is a public health and human rights issue. To combat it effectively, there must be an honest appraisal by Muslims of the influence of Muhammad's example here, and a forthright willingness to stand up and say that his example in this must not be followed today. Whether or not there is any hope that Muslims will actually do that in any significant group is another question, but if it is not done, it is certain that the problem will continue.

Bottom line: When Militant Islamists wage war in the name of Islam and claim to be following the example of Mohammed, it behooves the civilized world to shed some light on Islam and Mohammed. The truth is on our side in this effort. In taking up this battle, we gain key high ground in the information war.

So, I guess this answers why we can expect no help from the MSM in this battle.

11 August 2006

Where is Islam's Flight 93?

I was flying yesterday, and most people I came in contact with understood we are in a war. …

Every time I wonder and worry that people will forget the stakes, the enemy reminds us … 3/11 [3/1/04 Madrid, Spain train bombings] … 7/7 [7/7/05 London suicide attacks targeting public transportation] … Zarqawi [former leader of Al-Qaeda in Iraq], Zawahiri [Bin-Laden's #2 who often sent threatening messages during this period], etc.

Indeed, yesterday most people seemed to understand. They coughed up their lotions, liquids, and such. There were a few complaints, principally from women losing costly make-up and men who probably should have spent some time in the military in their younger days.

But people were generally in pretty good spirits. Flights were late, and lines were long.

People were discussing "profiling." I heard it on the radio, too. The consensus is rising to get serious and rational regarding the] threat we are facing. The Congress should address this … now.

Let's be frank. We've said it before. Certainly not all Muslims are terrorists. This is true, and thank God for it. There are great people in the Muslim world. In fact, it appears that some Muslim informants may have helped to break up the London plot.

But … but … virtually all terrorists are Muslims. This is a fact. It's an uncomfortable fact, but the world must face it.

Most normal people unencumbered by either politics or relations with politically-correct institutions have no difficulty in saying this.

We all know it. And we are only endangering ourselves if we don't approach our security honestly. To the extent Muslims don't like the fact that all terrorists are Muslims (or at least claim to be), then they need to police their own and tell us and the world why they are right and how the jihadis have "hijacked" the faith.

What I see is Muslims trying to hijack planes. And the Muslim hijackers claim that they are the true believers. They cite sacred texts to bolster their arguments, and the jihadis claim that Muslim "moderates" are the hijackers of the faith. And shock ... the moderates are not too aggressive in trying to "take back the faith." When a serious fight starts, who wants a moderate on their side?

Muslims who abhor terrorism had better get a hold of their faith. If it was indeed stolen by radicals, then how about some righteous indignation and fighting back against the jihadis who are tarnishing the name of Islam?

If Islam has indeed been hijacked by radicals, then where is Islam's Fight 93? ...

26 May 2006

United 93

I went to see United 93 simply because I had to. I was drawn to revisit the horrific savagery of Militant Islam unmasked, but I mainly wanted to see its antidote —the heroism of the heart of the free ... and the brave.

I went not quite knowing what to expect, but I was expecting a lot. The movie did not disappoint.

There was so much, from the eerie beginning where the jihadi pilot interrupts the morning prayers of his co-conspirators by announcing, "It is time," to the gut-wrenching conclusion where the plane plows into a Pennsylvania field ... with no sound.

My thoughts and emotions, swirling for two hours, filled the soundless void as I thought of the mothers, dads, loved ones, sweethearts, women murdered by the ruthless enemy that we now fight.

And fight we must. This is a central theme and inescapable conclusion that is powerfully delivered by the film.

As the events of 9/11 unfolded in the movie, I was struck by the unsung acts of heroism and professionalism as a free society scrambled to defend itself against a surprise attack by its totalitarian enemies. The chaos and emotional reality of this scramble for life was well-done in the movie. Only in history books is heroism and combat neat and clean.

The twists of this for-real plot are many. Inexplicably, the jihadis plan failed to account for the routine delay out of Newark on the morning of 9/11. United 93 was delayed about 40 minutes, as it often was, as the jihadis in first-class sweated it out. This delay in takeoff meant that that the United 93 strike —apparently meant for the U.S. capitol — would not be coordinated with the strikes at the World Trade Center and the Pentagon. Further, the jihadis failed to account for the likely use of … phones by passengers who could then be informed by people on the ground (thanks to the 24-hour news cycle) of the events of 9/11. Combining the foregoing, the jihadis did not account for the passengers' ability to learn the plot before it would be carried out.

Most importantly, though, the jihadis failed to account for the heart and heroism of a group of ordinary, randomly-assembled Americans.

The movie convinced me that Divine Providence intervened on United 93. For instance, flight attendants assisting a stabbed passenger managed to see both pilots in the front of plane lying on the floor and covered in blood. This image, when relayed to the passengers assembled in the rear of the plane, stirred momentary horror, but then action.

One passenger asked, "Who is flying the plane then?" If passengers believed that an American commercial pilot was flying the plane, then perhaps they would have gone quietly. This is apparently what occurred on the three other flights. Once the passengers realized that a jihadi was at the controls, though, the situation began to change on United 93.

As … phone calls went out to loved ones, the passengers learned the horrifying details of what was unfolding on 9/11. And then they began informing each other. By these myriad, desperate calls home, we have a good picture today of what unfolded on United 93.

Realizing that their plane would be used as a missile by the jihadi pilot, the decision to act was quickly reached by a group of men on the flight.

A plan was made, albeit it would be a long shot. There was a pilot on the plane (although with no jet or commercial experience) and an air traffic controller, too. The passengers hoped not simply to take the plane down, but to take it back from the suicidal jihadis. It was a long shot, but if it failed they would at least keep the plane from flying into an American target. Still, all realized that their prospects were grim.

A passenger with a foreign accent counseled against provoking the jihadis. He was overruled.

Crying passengers made final phone calls. This was hard to watch. The passengers were terrified in these final moments, but they proceeded with courage nonetheless.

Indeed, courage isn't the absence of fear but proceeding to do the right thing in the face of it.

And speaking of courage, men gathered in the back of the plane to arm themselves with makeshift weapons, such as forks, knives, a fire extinguisher, whatever. It was inspiring to watch their presence of mind and adaptability under such duress.

Then they spent a moment to reflect. The chaotic scene was hardly one for reflection, either. They made final calls.

Todd Beamer recited the Lord's prayer and prompted his fellow passengers with the now-famous, "Let's roll." Jeremy Glick, a 31-year-old Jewish man who happened to know judo ("I'll break his arm, like this ..."), led the attack.

As I was watching, I was reminded of how the jihadis can only prevail when they have the element of complete surprise. ... They are weak. The passengers of United 93 exposed them as such.

And surprise only carries you so far. ... Furthermore, it is operationally impossible to maintain the element of surprise at each stage of a long conflict. If you are going to need surprise for victory, you must deliver a knockout blow. But the jihadis are incapable of such a blow.

As the men came up the aisle, knife-wielding jihadis were taken down and a drink cart became a battering ram to break down the cockpit door. Inside the cockpit, the jihadi pilot realized that his mission was finished ... and would fail. He had placed a picture of the capitol on the stick.

The passengers ultimately reached the cockpit and then got their hands on the pilot. Then the plane came down.

As United 93 approached Washington, there were no planes in

the area with shoot-down authority. That is, but for the heroism of the passengers aboard United 93, the plane would have almost certainly slammed into the capitol at nearly 600 mph.

Though the government was not ready yet to respond, its people were already engaged in the battle. America's first fighting unit of the post-9/11 world had been randomly-assembled on a commercial flight. And these ordinary Americans, without even a former member of the military among the group that stormed the cockpit, planned and mounted their own surprise attack.

Steeped in backward radicalism, prejudice and completely ignorant of American history, it's understandable that the totalitarian, jihadi mind would fail to anticipate meeting a man like Tom Burnett on United 93. …

The film depicts Tom Burnett as leading the planning of the passenger assault on the cockpit. Here is what Burnett told his wife in his last phone call to her: "We're all going to die, but three of us are going to do something." Then he signed off: "I love you, honey."

Shortly after his final words to his wife, Burnett and his fellow passengers won the first engagement of the post-9/11 world. …

DC Shutdown: National security—defending America against all enemies foreign and domestic—is a critical component of my political philosophy, a key strand in the cord without which the whole cord breaks. And, to its credit, the Bush Administration, while failing to engage in the information war, did aggressively pursue America's enemies. On the domestic front, however, the breach between the Republican Establishment and the party's base (which has now largely become the "Deplorables" who support Pres. Trump) was exposed for all to see when Pres. Bush nominated his friend Harriet Miers to the Supreme Court. In doing so, Pres. Bush's establishment bona fides were solidified while some of his most ardent supporters like myself were thus put in the awkward position of having to fight the disastrous Miers nomination. The next chapter details this transformational showdown.

Chapter Five:

Brushed back by the Establishment

Getting up and Defeating the Harriet Miers Nomination to the Supreme Court

3 October 2005

His WH Counsel Harriet Miers?

What? Are you kidding me?

In case you are wondering ... yes, I am shocked and completely disappointed. Unless someone somewhere knows something huge that I don't, there is no way to spin this pick for the Supreme Court by Pres. Bush other than a huge mistake.

And perhaps a betrayal of those of us who have worked so hard to elect him President ... twice.

A justice like Scalia? Thomas? Please.

Harry Reid approves of her? That makes me feel better.

I am going to gather some more information before giving my final answer.

But this morning I am saying: This nominee should have been Judge Edith Jones. And Judge Jones' age (56), thought to be a liability, is not when compared to the 60-year-old Miers.

By all indications, a terrible pick. Worse than that, a pick based upon no qualifications but only cronyism. And don't blow smoke in an orifice not intended for such a use by telling me she is the best person for the job. Jones, Luttig, Alito, Corrigan, McConnell and Garza are out there ... and we get Miers? What?!

At least the spineless Republicans in the Senate preserved the filibuster. I may filibuster this pick.

Update: Still steaming ... here is a comment of mine over at confirmthem.com:

"Pres. Bush, who seems to understand the need to stand and fight on the international stage doesn't get it on the domestic front. ... His enemies will be emboldened and his friends ... it's inaccurate to say they will be depressed ... they are completely deflated. Why fight for this crap?

When you have the Senate, the House ... had, I should say ... unbelievable. Maybe this proves that the parties are really no different as some have been saying."

3 October 2005

I was Conservative when Conservative wasn't Cool

... If you have read this blog much (yeah, both of you), you will note that I have not once posted anything here that could be construed as negative of Pres. Bush. I vigorously supported his election and re-election. I gave my time and money to same. This is nothing new for me.

Remember Barbara Mandrell's song "I was Country When Country Wasn't Cool?" It was popular when I was in high school here in Texas. A lot of "Urban Cowboys" were born then. Me? I just stayed the same. I was never much of a cowboy, even though I am a native Houstonian.

Once I became a Christian in 1978, my world view changed. I began to see how things fit together. No one told me how to think. I discovered that I was a conservative. The world view began to knit together. I came to love and admire Pres. Ronald Reagan. I cast my first vote in a presidential election in 1984 ... for Pres. Reagan. I have voted in every election since. I have supported many, many Republicans and a few conservative Democrats along the way, but my voting record has been consistent —conservative.

I have been in the ideological trenches for 25 years now. Yes, I was conservative when conservative wasn't cool. I remain, as I always have been, a conservative first and a Republican second. There are still many Republicans whom I admire and support, and on the whole, the party is far closer to my views than the Democrats. Not even close. The Constitution Party, Pat Buchanites, and other members of the "Perfect Church and Counting Angels on Heads of Pins" crowd don't appeal to me.

I believe in winning. I am a pragmatist. I believe in compromise to build majorities. I like to smile and laugh. I like to be "for" things. ...

Have you ever noticed that justices don't drift right? Do they just get "smarter" and more liberal? Please.

Some are touting her evangelical faith. As an evangelical, let me just say: 1) This is humorous; and 2) I did not fall off the proverbial turnip truck. Note this political rule: If you mention your faith as a positive, you are generally not a conservative. I am also sure that Jesse Jackson would claim that he supports life and loves Jesus, too. Heck, he probably does. What are we nominating? A deaconess? An ABA President?

And by the way, this Texan doesn't care that she is from Texas. A conservative American would do just fine.

We could have done so much better. Judges Jones, Luttig, Janice Rogers Brown, Alito, McConnell, Corrigan, etc. I feel badly for each of them, especially Judge Edith Jones of the Fifth Circuit. The only negative from conservatives (other than a difficult confirmation fight, and I believe this could actually be a positive) for Judge Jones was her age — 56. She is four years younger than Harriet Miers. This hurts.

Now, we have to guess and hope. And a great opportunity for an informative debate (and one that conservatives would win) is lost.

This nomination is just plain a bad idea on all fronts. It smacks of defeatism and of a lame-duck presidency. It needs to be withdrawn and/or defeated. I am hoping for someone to step up and come with me.

Because this conservative still is conservative —whether the Republican-first crowd thinks it is cool or not.

4 October 2005

More Miers: Gasp! There's a Naked Person in the Room

The crowd cheering the Miers nomination is like the people cheering about the infamous Emperor's new clothes. ...

For the Republican-first-at-all-cost crowd who has not been paying attention for the last 20 years, there is a huge, important debate over the role of the judiciary in this country that has been needed since Robert Bork was destroyed in 1987. The Roberts hearings did not provide this opportunity, because the Demos wisely backed away. Everyone knows that the real battle is with the next nominee. That is, the next nominee will carry the standard. Yet, Pres. Bush has strangely put forth a stealth nominee whose credentials are questioned. These are legitimate questions, too. Thus, even if Harriet Miers were the person to wage this battle —and I doubt this —she will have lost it before it has begun.

Yet, some are complaining at those of us who gasped at the sight of the naked emperor. The Democrats know. In spite of their initial warm statements (and why wouldn't they be so warm with such an easy target), they are trying to destroy this President. He has thrown them ammunition to do so. Friends like me protested and "gasped." Now, we are the problem?

The first Pres. Bush foolishly believed the Demos when he "cooperated" with them in raising taxes. The current Pres. Bush will get savaged by his enemies as well if he doesn't wake up soon and withdraw this nomination.

7 October 2005

As if it weren't obvious enough ...

The Miers nomination is doomed, check out this nugget [from the *Washington Post*]:

> While generally well received, Miers has had a
> few awkward moments, including one during her
> Wednesday session with Sen. Patrick J. Leahy

(Vt.), ranking Democrat on the Judiciary Committee.

In an initial chat with Miers, according to several people with knowledge of the exchange, Leahy asked her to name her favorite Supreme Court justices. Miers responded with "Warren" —which led Leahy to ask her whether she meant former Chief Justice Earl Warren, a liberal icon, or former Chief Justice Warren Burger, a conservative who voted for *Roe v. Wade*. Miers said she meant Warren Burger, the sources said.

So, we can glean from this that 1) Miers likes Earl Warren; or 2) she, unlike every other lawyer in America, likes and respects Warren Burger ... no wait, he is her favorite justice of all time; and/or 3) she is on a first-name basis with "Warren"; and/or 4) she is not smart at all; and/or 5) she is liberal.

At least 2 or 3 of the foregoing not-so-good things appear to be true. However, one thing is for sure from the aforementioned exchange with Leahy: She is not for overruling *Roe v. Wade*.

I am so glad the President saw her heart. ...

8 October 2005

Have I said anything about Harriet Miers lately?

It has been informative, inspiring and entertaining to participate in the raging debate at confirmthem.com. Lots of insight, information and wit ... with of course some gallows humor and irreverence mixed in. How can any feeling of reverence be associated with this disaster? (That is a rhetorical question, class.)

As a great example of the type of argument that the shills just shove aside with "Trust Me," check out this comment by "Insider:"

Let's review, shall we:

1. Her favorite Justice is "Earl…Warren…Burger"(?)
2. She "toned" down a WH Christmas message
    because it was "too Christian"(?!)

3. She set up a liberal lecture series at SMU.
4. She donated money to Al Gore AND the DNC.
5. She spoke out in favor of affirmative action quotas while she was at the Dallas City Council.
6. She presided over ABA meetings where official favorable ABA positions in regards to the International Crime Court and gay adoption were decided.
7. Bush named 4 persons to the Texas Supreme Court between 1994-2000, including Gonzo, while he named Miers….to the Texas Lottery Commission.
8. [She] expressed dismay about the "federalist society types" Gonzo had put in place at the Counsel's Office (further comments unfavorable about federalist society also available at the Knight Ridder newspapers recent article).

Sounds like a "mainstream nominee" ... from the Clinton administration. …

Note: Miers was apparently dismayed by the very same Federalist Society that Pres. Trump leaned heavily on in formulating the conservative judicial nominations that helped propel him to victory in 2016.

8 October 05

The Godfather calls for a hit.

Bork says Miers Pick a "disaster on every level."

With all due respect to Nickie Goomba, The Godfather of the conservative legal movement calls for a "hit" on Miers.

Here's Don Bork beating around the bush, as usual [in a recent interview with Tucker Carlson]:

> I think it's a disaster on every level. ... [T]his is a woman who's undoubtedly as wonderful a person as they say she is, but so far as anyone can

tell she has no experience with constitutional law whatever. Now it's a little late to develop a constitutional philosophy or begin to work it out when you're on the court already. So that—I'm afraid she's likely to be influenced by factors, such as personal sympathies and so forth, that she shouldn't be influenced by. I don't expect that she can be, as the president says, a great justice. But the other level is more worrisome, in a way: it's kind of a slap in the face to the conservatives who've been building up a conservative legal movement for the last 20 years.

Clearly, he is just an elitist, or a liberal, or a sexist ... or maybe just not on the WH payroll or trying to get invited to the White House.

10 October 2005

A Liberal Understands the Republican Base Better than the White House

Via confirmthem.com, we learn of a liberal who understands the stakes in the Miers pick. Said liberal is Rogers Cadenhead. ...The liberal is spot on in this instance, and here is his take:

> Stealth nominees have a strategic short-term advantage that makes it difficult to keep them off the court, so it's likely that Miers will be confirmed unless President Bush withdraws the nomination, which ranks in probability somewhere between "no chance in hell" and "never in a million years." The president's so stubborn that were he captain of the Titanic, he would have run the ship into a second iceberg to prove he meant to hit the first one.
>
> There's a long-term price for filling the Supreme Court in secrecy ... . Conservatives

have built an intellectual foundation for their interpretation of constitutional law over a quarter century, as embodied by the Federalist Society and the embrace of originalism.

Neither Bush appointment has publicly nurtured this movement during their careers. In some instances, they've even distanced themselves from it. When asked her most admired Supreme Court justice, Miers did not choose Justices Scalia or Thomas. When John Roberts showed up in a Federalist Society membership directory, the White House issued a quick denial, stating that he "has no recollection of being a member."

Roger Pilon, a Cato Institute vice president and society member, was stunned to see Roberts run away from the association as if Joseph McCarthy was after him. "Are you now, or have you ever been, a member of the Federalist Society?"

If you're a 25-year-old conservative who graduated Harvard Law first in your class and clerks for Chief Justice Roberts, do you spend the next 20 years contributing to law journals, actively participating in the Federalist Society and seeking a judgeship from which you can foster conservative jurisprudence?

Clearly, if you have supreme ambitions, the answer is no. By choosing Roberts and Miers, Bush has publicly affirmed the notion that judicial conservatives believe in an ideology that dare not speak its name. Friends of Clarence are the new Friends of Dorothy, forced to develop furtive code phrases to seek each other out—just like how President Bush namedrops Dred Scott as a double-secret shout out to anti-abortion activists.

"I couldn't help but overhear what you said about *Griswold v. Connecticut* at the bar, friend. Want to take this someplace more private so we can disrespect stare decisis away from all of these living constitutionalists?"

Harriet Miers is the best thing to happen to liberals since the repeal of anti-sodomy laws. I hope she has a sister.

The liberals have spoken. They love this nomination.

Cadenhead unwittingly, though, makes a more fundamental point: The Left expects more of conservatives than the sneaking "strategery" involved in the Miers nomination. They are loathe to admit this, but they hold us to a higher standard. Yes, I did notice and thank you, Mr. Cadenhead.

Liberals expect intellectual honesty from us, and generally they get it. We in the conservative movement have never been unashamed of conservative jurisprudence. Why should we be? We are winning the debate against unprincipled judges who substitute their liberal policy preferences that would never succeed at the ballot box. We are succeeding on every front, from the court of public opinion to the halls of academia. Virtually every law school in the country talks disdainfully about how *Roe v. Wade* is a contradictory, result-oriented decision on a collision-course with technology and medical science.

Why is it then, that the White House is ashamed of the Federalist Society, which was co-founded by one of the justices that Pres. Bush claims to admire? Why does the White House act like nominating a conservative to the Supreme Court is the equivalent of nominating a member of the Taliban? Don't they understand that this emboldens liberals and legitimizes their arguments that mainstream conservatives are in fact out of Chuck Schumer's "mainstream?"

One possible answer: The White House is not really that conservative, after all. If you think the WH is really a conservative White House, I would like to hear the evidence. We conservative peasants outside the establishmentarians' palace are getting restless.

11 October 2005

The Most Compelling Case for Miers Yet: The Evangelical and the Atheist

Came across a column and a post tonight that are, in my view, worthy of your attention.

First, I have been watching carefully to see the take on the Miers nomination by my "Hero Professor" and fellow evangelical, Dr. Marvin Olasky of the University of Texas. I took Dr. Olasky's journalism history class at Texas, and I have been a fan of his ever since. This brilliant, yet humble and gracious man is a former Marxist and Boston Globe reporter (he says he fit right in) turned evangelical Christian. He is also the author of Compassionate Conservatism, yes, the book that inspired the President's campaign theme.

Currently editor-in-chief of World Magazine, he still works as a token conservative journalism professor at UT.

… Dr. O makes the most persuasive case for the confirmation of Harriet Miers to date. … Here is the passage [in his column] that really struck me for its insight and connecting of dots:

> … Columnist Michelle Malkin argues well that "a good heart does not a great Supreme Court justice make." No, but it might make a person remain an originalist.
>
> Heart: In so many ways, this appointment is classic Bush. Nearly six years ago, when asked in an early debate among Republican presidential candidates to name his favorite philosopher, W. famously said, "Christ, because he changed my heart." The pooh-poohing of his answer then (favorite philosopher —the

question was about mind, not heart) anticipated the current debate among conservatives: Suffering servant? Why not intellectual leader?

It's George W. Bush's analysis that "heart" is crucial, since a good mind by itself also does not a great justice make. We may end up having been bamboozled by this nominee, in which case the Republican Party will pay a heavy price. But give Bush credit for going beyond the assumption that the person who would be the best constitutional law professor makes the best nominee. He has not only nominated a justice, but implicitly called for a paradigm shift in conservative thinking.

What Dr. O is saying is that he has concluded that the President has concluded that Harriet Miers faith will keep her faithful to an originalist approach to the Constitution. That is, her integrity (which is grounded in her faith) will keep her steady in her originalist approach to the Constitution. Okay, this I understand. And I also understand the reluctance to market this for MSM dissemination.

So then, in the interest of fairness, what do the atheists have to say? Well, it just so happens that one of my favorite atheists, UT's Constitutional Law professor Lino Graglia, was interviewed by "WH Communications Director" Hugh Hewitt today.

Full disclosure: Graglia is another old professor of mine, and he may be the funniest professor ever. For example, he would occasionally make fun of liberal students' hair to conclude a debate/discussion. This was not received well, except by right-minded types such as myself. The cynical conservatism of this Brooklyn native is highlighted by one of his favorite anecdotes: "Liberals wake up every morning and ask, 'What good can I do today?' Me? I just wake up and say, "Thank God my throat wasn't cut last night."

The Graglia interview with Hewitt was great, and I was shocked to see that Graglia said the following: "Nathan Hecht is very trustworthy.

Nathan Hecht is probably the most conservative judge on the Texas Supreme Court, very trustworthy. He speaks very highly of Miers, who he knows, and that is a large part of my basis of belief that she'll be all right." Yet, Graglia also does sympathize with conservatives' "Souterphobia." And he asks "the" question: "The Supreme Court is running the country. What point electing conservatives if you don't change that?"

Exactly.

So, still fuming over the mismanagement of this debacle and the assault on those of us who would dare question this nomination, I am at least heartened by the confidence in Miers I see coming from Olasky and Graglia. Maybe this nomination, if it succeeds, won't be the disaster that Judge Bork fears.

So, the believer Olasky and the athiest Graglia have come together. What in the world could be next?

How about some patience with us agnostics?

Note: The foregoing post was linked by Hugh Hewitt, a nationally-syndicated talk radio host with the Salem Radio Network on October 11, 2005 (hughhewitt.com/page/3062 Oct. 11, 2005), with the following comment: "Daisy Cutter has mellowed a bit as well, and though I am not the 'White House Communications Director' as he suggests, I am pleased to have provided the Graglia interview that moved him a bit." For reasons that will become clear in the posts that follow, however, this was the last time Daisy Cutter was either linked or mentioned by Hewitt (though he had linked to the blog on at least one occasion previously). The ultimate establishmentarian, Hewitt was determined to remain on the USS Miers until the bitter, and I do mean bitter, end.

12 October 2005

A Friend Like Nathan

Speaking out about/against/skeptically about the Miers nomination is for me somewhat like Nathan confronting David.

So, I am prophet? Hardly. My point is: I remain a friend and

supporter of the President. But he made a mistake here and a biggee —
even if Harriet Miers is a Thomas or Scalia (which I still doubt).

Many of the President's most ardent supporters —that would be
conservatives like me —are up in arms and fit to be tied. Now, we read
that Republican staff lawyers on the Senate Judiciary Committee are
participating in the revolt. The First Lady clumsily and, yes, outrageously
deals the "possibly sexism" card. Miers supporters threaten political
Armageddon if we don't toe the line; Miers opponents threaten
Armageddon, as well.

Sounds like if the confrontation continues, it's going to be
Armageddon either way, no? So, this is how we get the big "fight" over
judges ... not with the Democrats, but with conservatives? Oh, the irony.

Indeed, the mother of all confirmation battles, a battle that will
sap the President of whatever fading political capital he may have left,
looms. And no matter the results, all will be left feeling like losers.

So, what to do? How can Armageddon be avoided in a way that
preserves the integrity of all concerned?

I have a suggestion. Caveat: Please ignore the following
suggestion, unless you believe Harriet Miers is the only confirmable
person in America who would fulfill the President's promise to nominate
justices in the mold of Scalia or Thomas. Oh, wait ... I forgot. Tex. Sen.
John Cornyn, who knows her well, says "she is no Scalia or Thomas."
Scratch that. Okay, here's my suggestion to avert Republican
Armageddon: Maybe it's time for Harriet Miers to be a true friend to the
President and tell him the hard truth: This pick is an honor and I thank
you. But it's not helping your agenda, our party, or the country. I
withdraw.

12 October 2005

DC's Law of Supreme Court Inertia

As I was telling my buddy and convinced Miers believer Don Surber,
you gotta understand the Law of Supreme Court Inertia. It goes like this:
Justices at rest, whether they be liberal or conservative, tend to stay at
rest. Justices in motion ... tend to drift left.

Hence, without evidence of "mooring" such as to define a justice's jurisprudential location, we must always assume that justices will drift. And when the inevitable storm surge of pressure comes, the unmoored will surely drift. And they always drift left.

13 October 2005

Unbelievable

I have tried/wanted to keep an open mind after initial shock and disappointment over the Miers nomination. The confidence of my former professors Marvin Olasky and Lino Graglia gave me some pause. Meanwhile, I have withstood the inane, vapid arguments in favor of the nomination (don't worry, just trust ... it'll be okay) combined with and attacks on the conservative base by certain Miers supporters.

Our ol' buddy Hugh Hewitt supposedly comforts conservatives by saying that Miers will be like Potter "I know it when I see it" Stewart. Beam me up. This is too much to take. Is this real, or is it "Harriet Potter"?

Does anyone have the transcript where Pres. Bush promised nominees like ... Potter Stewart? What?!

No more. I am opposed. No turning back.

Miers' defenders have tried to explain her apparent disdain for my beloved Federalist Society (I let my membership lapse long ago, but I am renewing now), which to me has been a huge red flag. ...

Harriet Miers, it is time for you to do the loyal and right thing. Please withdraw.

14 October 2005

If you think conservatives are outraged over the Miers nomination ...

Take a look at evangelicals. A fascinating Pew Research poll shows 54% of conservative Republicans in favor of the Miers nomination, while only 43% of evangelicals support the nomination. Another 41% of evangelicals have no opinion and the rest are like me ... opposed. ...

So, what gives? Well, it is pretty simple, but frankly it helps to be one of "them" to understand. Recall Clarence Thomas? He was overwhelmingly disapproved of by the black community. Why would only the second black man to serve on the SC be viewed so unfavorably by the black community? Simple. He is a conservative.

As for Miers, the same analysis applies. Most evangelicals are conservatives. Miers may or may not be a conservative, but she has no demonstrably conservative judicial philosophy. Additionally, most evangelicals don't support special favors or quotas. So, they don't approve of a nomination just because "one of them" was nominated.

Add on top of this the fact that a number of prominent evangelicals have spoken in favor of Miers and the poll numbers are even more striking. …

And prominent evangelical bloggers such as Hugh Hewitt are too busy selling the WH line: "Trust me. Be quiet. Wait. Be loyal now. Don't you know the sky will fall, the country will be destroyed, and evangelicals will revolt if she is rejected?" This is laughable …

You know, I know evangelicals. I know me. The truth is that most of my Christian friends are just scratching their heads over this pick and saying things to me like, "Huh?" or "What in the world is he thinking?" …

As for me, I've got my smile back on … There's a deep satisfaction in standing up for what is right, because no matter the ultimate outcome you've already won.

17 October 2005

DC Rules: Hugh Hewitt Not Guilty of Fraud but Guilty of Incoherence and Inconsistency

… You should know that I like and respect Hugh Hewitt. Nothing herein is meant as a personal attack. But Hugh has really got it wrong on the Miers nomination, in my judgment. I think it is important to expose his faulty logic and reasoning. You can decide for yourself and act accordingly.

Over the weekend, a diarist at *RedState* posted the

following "smoking gun" regarding the arguments made by Hewitt before Harriet Miers was nominated. …

In addition to arguing that the nominee should be closer to 50 than 60, Hugh said:

> You see, I've tried to explain to people about Judge Janice Rogers Brown, that she has not been a federal judge. And my concern over her and Priscilla Owen is, that federal judges just do different things than state judges. And I want to see a little bit from them, before you run as a conservative. I don't want to run blind. And I think she really hasn't done, for example, federalism issues, hasn't done federal pre-emption, hasn't interpreted the free exercise of the establishment clause, though there are Constitutional counterparts in California. That's my concern .... I just don't think they're reliable enough when it comes to understanding how they'll handle federal issues.

I mean, but couldn't we just "trust the President" before 10/3 in the same way we could post-10/3, Hugh? Maybe not.

And then Hugh argued the following:

> And brilliance matters, even if you're a dissent, because you've got to mold the law schools. You've got to mold the professions. You've got to look ahead. I think Bush needs to go for someone about whom there is no question of intellectual...the capacity for intellectual greatness.

If I were a Miers supporter, perhaps I would argue that Hugh's position was "elitist." But no, it was just pre-10/3/05 [when Miers was nominated]. And I think he was telling the truth then. And he was right. And after perusing Miers vacuous ruminations in *the* Texas Bar Journal, let there be no more pretending that Miers is some brilliant scholar.

Suffice it to say, we haven't heard such arguments (about the need for brilliance and/or a track record) from Hugh since 10/3. Yet, we have heard plenty of similar arguments from the critics of the Miers nomination —people such as myself …

Dissecting Hugh's Defense

Not surprisingly, Hugh response concludes with, and ultimately rests upon, the "Trust me" theme: "But the field is large, many forces are at work on it only a few of which I glimpse, and President Bush has not broken his word on a promise to his party yet."

A few weeks ago, I would have said the same. Indeed, most of the conservative angst at Pres. Bush is not over the fact that he has broken promises, but over the fact that that he has not governed as a conservative. For example, understandable conservative concern over immigration is not as a result of Pres. Bush breaking a promise. He has always been strangely silent about the growing immigration problem. Furthermore, he promised he would pass medicare reform that included prescription drug coverage. I wasn't excited about this promise during the campaign, but you can't say he didn't keep his word on this score. Recall, too, that he said he would govern as a "compassionate conservative," but he never defined the term. Others were left to speculate what this might mean.

However, fast forward to this dispute: The President clearly promised (albeit without using those precise words) to nominate judges in the mold of Scalia and Thomas. So, conservatives have rightly asked if Harriet Miers fits this description. Meanwhile, we have been troubled by statements such as those by Texas Sen. John Cornyn: "She is no Scalia and Thomas." Well, maybe Sen. Cornyn is wrong or means something other than the plain meaning of the words themselves (an ironic twist in this debate, for sure). Maybe I should just be inclined to give the President the benefit of the doubt. Maybe I would …

But a recent column by George Will pointed out something to me that I had frankly forgotten. In recent years, Will has worn thin as he has seemed all-too-ready to try his "independent" wings. But I read the column and was persuaded by it. Why? Because facts are stubborn things. Here is the passage that really struck me:

> In addition, the president has forfeited his right to be trusted as a custodian of the Constitution. The forfeiture occurred March 27, 2002, when, in a private act betokening an uneasy conscience, he signed the McCain-Feingold law expanding government regulation of the timing, quantity and content of political speech. The day before the 2000 Iowa caucuses he was asked —to ensure a considered response from him, he had been told in advance that he would be asked — whether McCain-Feingold's core purposes are unconstitutional. He unhesitatingly said, "I agree." Asked if he thought presidents have a duty, pursuant to their oath to defend the Constitution, to make an independent judgment about the constitutionality of bills and to veto those he thinks unconstitutional, he briskly said, "I do."

Again, think what you may of Will, but facts are facts.

I knew Pres. Bush opposed the disastrous McCain Campaign Finance "Reform" —a measure that has now spread its perniciousness tentacles even into the blogosphere —but I thought the President signed it to avert a showdown with McCain and to preserve precious "political capital." Well, it turns out the President did just that, but he also broke a promise in the process.

And he broke a promise at the core of the Miers debate —Can we trust the President to be faithful to a conservative understanding of the Constitution? My answer now is: Perhaps we can, but I want to be able to verify for myself whether Miers is in fact a conservative in the mold of Scalia or Thomas. To date, there is no evidence to support this assertion. In fact, the evidence is that Miers is an indecisive woman who has changed her views in various roles and stages of her life. She has espoused liberal opinions on multiple occasions and in multiple decades, but the President brazenly and almost humorously says, "I know she'll be the same in 20 years." I won't chronicle all of Miers' zigging and zagging here, but there is considerable doubt that she is in fact a fulfillment of Pres. Bush's campaign commitment.

If during the campaign the President had said he would nominate people like Harriet Miers to the SC, how many people would not have voted for him?

As for Hugh, the problem with his position is not that he has now —his previous comments notwithstanding —decided for political reasons to support the nomination. The problem is what he and the WH's other supporters have said about those of us who disagree with the very same arguments that Hugh made pre-10/3.

To those who have argued about Miers that "brilliance matters" post-10/3, Hugh and the WH have said that we are "elitist," indeed part of the dreaded "Bos-Wash axis of elitism." That is a nice ad hominem swipe aimed to knock us Miers opponents all the way to the middle of a Red State wipeout. But, come on, Hugh. I live in the capitol of Red State America —Texas.

Recall, too, that Hugh has also intimated that there is a "hint" of anti-evangelicalism in the air, as well. And this "anti-evangelicalism" stems from ... you guessed it ... elitism. And Hugh has warned of an "evangelical backlash" against the "elites" if Miers is not confirmed. ...

In sum, the common theme in Hugh's arguments has been that opponents of the Miers nomination have had improper motives—elitism, anti-evangelicalism, etc. He has pulled no punches, stating the Miers opponents were engaging in the "big sulk," were behaving like "Kos Kids," were "D.C. druids," and when questioning the resume of Harriet Miers were engaging in a course of conduct of no utility and "zero honor."

If I were Andy Card, perhaps I'd call such arguments "cynical" or worse. But I'm not Andy Card. I'm just a conservative Christian from Texas. So, I will simply say that Hugh's just wrong, and he's grasping at straws. And dare I say it? Yes, he's calling names because his argument is so very weak.

The fact is that conservatives skeptical of the Miers pick are simply making the case for "brilliance" and for a conservative track record. Herein lies Hugh's problem: It is fine for him to argue that his position changed. But it is inconsistent or incoherent to impute bad motives to those making the same arguments he has recently made.

To top all of this off, Hugh's credibility on the Miers nomination was forever tarnished by his gushing statement on October 3 that Miers was a "solid, B+ pick". Recalling from the grading scale, if "A" is excellent, and "B" is good, that would make Hugh the only person in America who believes this is a very good pick (except for Laura "Those Who Disagree are Possibly Sexists" Bush). Yet, I think he knows this is not the case. And I don't think he's misrepresenting here, either. … I just think that Hugh is so inclined to give the Republicans a pass that he just has a hard time seeing the truth. Hugh takes the sympathetic argument —my country, right or wrong —and mutates it to "my party, right or wrong." I am unwilling to go this far.

The truth is that, through the rosiest of rose-colored glasses, this was a "C-" pick. Hugh should have said so, and in the process would not have lost so much credibility in this debate. I will be charitable and give the pick a "D." After all, it has only shattered conservative confidence in the President and emboldened his opponents, while potentially taking a 30-year opportunity to reshape the Court and instead turning it into a colossal disappointment. Even if Miers turns out great (again, I very much doubt this) the path to her appointment to the bench will likely be littered with political casualties —Republican and/or conservative ones.

The Verdict

In reaching my conclusion, I found this this jewel from Hugh, written on October 2, the eve of the Miers' nomination:

> In the end, I am hoping that President Bush
> makes a choice that he can defend to the country
> as a simple merit pick, free of political calculation
> or constituency bolstering. Very few, if any,
> serious ConLaw scholars would debate the
> intellectual qualifications of either man [Luttig or
> McConnell], and their colleagues from the

Reagan Executive Branch, the law school community or the bench will sing their praises. Either will be opposed as too conservative, which is simply outrageous partisanship. So there will be a fight, and the GOP has the votes to win.

There has never been a filibuster of a SCOTUS nominee over the perception of how he or she would vote. If the Senate Democrats mount such an effort, the country will get a very clear lesson in how unhinged that party's leadership has become from the country's political history and mainstream, and the Senate will have to vote on whether the filibuster can be applied to SCOTUS nominees. The Republicans will win that debate and that vote.

When the battle is over, and five and ten and twenty and perhaps even thirty years later, George W. Bush will be able to confidently assess his first two nominees to the SCOTUS and know that he did exactly the right thing for the right reasons.

The Supreme Court deserves the best jurists available to it. If the Constitution matters, then the nominees to join the court that interprets the Constitution should be those judges with the best intellectual talent, calm temperament and governmental experience.

Wow. Couldn't have said it better myself.

The only difference between Hugh and the legion of furious conservatives is that we are still making the arguments Hugh was making on 10/2. Hugh changed course on 10/3, as is his right. I am sure he has reasons for trusting the President's judgment. As I have said, people that I know and respect are doing the same.

But aren't the Miers opponents entitled to the same deference?

Indeed, it is wrong to castigate those of us who want the same for our Supreme Court today that we wanted before the Miers' pick.

21 October 2005

The Miers Nomination Continues to Flounder

… Recall that this brouhaha was supposed to fade after a couple of days as conservatives "got in line." Someone forgot to read the memo: Conservatives are not Demo-like, Bill Clinton-worshipping shills. …

The key here that is lost on Miers proponents is that this is not about the strategy or style of the two camps. This pick stinks now, and it will continue to stink. When you have a bad argument, there are just so many ways to dress it up. It's hard to fool a large number of people over an extended period of time. It is particularly hard to fool smart, committed conservatives. The longer this goes, the worse it will get for the Miers camp. …

This central point seems lost on the Miers pom-pom wavers: WE HAVE BEEN TOLD SUCH THINGS ABOUT JUDGES BEFORE, I.E., THEY ARE PRO-LIFE AND THESE BELIEFS STEM FROM STRONGLY-HELD RELIGIOUS BELIEFS. TRY THIS ON SOMEONE ELSE.

We need to know how they view the Constitution, not what their personal preferences are. Show us the money, i.e., the judicial philosophy in action, before a SC appointment was contemplated. Pardon me, but doesn't a conservative judge promise to put aside his or her personal preferences to faithfully rule on the case before him, anyway? Indeed, we want to see for ourselves and know that we are getting a true judicial conservative on the bench, someone who will be as faithful to the Constitution in 20 years as Scalia and Thomas are today. …

Party matters, Hugh, but it's not the only matter. I mean, if it were the only matter, then all the Senate RINOs would certainly play ball and vote for a real judicial conservative. Right? Well, liberal and conservative matter, too. …

Note: "Doesn't a conservative judge promise to put aside his or her personal preferences to faithfully rule on the case before him, anyway?" This is the exact tack taken by Pres. Trump's first two nominees to the Supreme Court, and campaigning with a list of potential conservative nominees was one of the key factors the propelled Trump to victory, easing concerns of some that as president Trump would govern as a conservative. Meanwhile many establishmentarians and purportedly conservative NeverTrumpers thought it would be better if Hillary Clinton had won the election (and appointed at least two Supreme Court justices). Go figure.

27 October 2005
Harriet Miers withdraws.

My initial response? This was a dignified, smart, and classy move by her and the White House. I wish Ms. Miers the best, and also I am hoping and praying the White House gets the next pick right. … I feel badly for Ms. Miers, but frankly she shouldn't have been in the situation she was in. Mostly though, I am proud to have stood with many conservatives in asking President Bush to stand by his campaign promise. …

DC Shutdown: By opposing the Miers nomination and the Republican Establishment, the sky did not fall. To the contrary, Justice Sam Alito was confirmed to the Supreme Court on January 31, 2006; he has been stellar. In the process of the Miers fight, the Republican base showed both it wants to win and also it can win by sticking to its core principles. In that regard, the next chapter explores some of the core legal issues that motivate conservatives and Christians to support Pres. Trump—namely, ensuring that our courts are free from political bias, in general, and chipping away at *Roe v. Wade* and other examples of arbitrary, judge-made law, in particular.

Chapter Six

I Fought the Law and the Truth Won

22 January 2005

Roe v. Wade Anniversary Reflections …
The Right to Talk about The Right to Life

This night I write on the issue of abortion. I hope these thoughts are received in the spirit in which they are intended, for I have learned that this most-contentious issue is indeed viewed differently by people of goodwill. I understand this, and even though the Supreme Court has essentially barred the subject from any meaningful legislative debate, we must still discuss it. Ironically, *Roe v. Wade* means that the nation must confront the issue even more.

It is indeed true that the views of most pro-lifers stem from their religious views. This is nothing new, and it certainly shouldn't disqualify the views from getting a hearing in the public square. What is not understood is that the other side also draws its firmly held convictions often from its view of God and morality, as well. The question then is: Who is right? As for me, I believe that life begins at conception and that every human life is sacred. … Life is a miracle, a precious gift. Some of you don't agree that life begins at conception, and I understand that. I respect your right to hold that belief.

However, do people who call themselves "pro-choice" respect my choices and beliefs on this issue? I haven't met many. And does our political system respect those who hold pro-life views? Sadly, it does not.

My pro-life views stem from my Christian faith. You need not share my faith to respect the pro-life position, however. You certainly need not share my faith to at least acknowledge that the issue is worthy of discussion and debate. There is much to be said for allowing our legislative process to address the issue of abortion.

Roe v. Wade: Judicial legislation inside a constitutional mirage.

Abortion rights were certainly not intended or contemplated by the framers of the Constitution. I have heard a number of constitutional scholars discuss the issue, and I have never heard one argue that abortion rights were intended by the framers. Indeed, all of the states outlawed the practice when the Bill of Rights was ratified. Further, all of the states continued to forbid abortions when the 14th Amendment (through which the Bill of Rights has been subsequently applied to the states) was ratified. In fact, the absence of abortion rights in the Constitution led the Supreme Court to incredibly resort to looking to the "penumbra" of the Constitution to find this right. *Roe v. Wade* is a terribly-written opinion that amounts to seven justices forcing their view of abortion rights upon the nation as a whole. The decision further created a collision course for itself, as the Court found abortion rights in the "penumbra" only until an unborn child is "viable." Medical science thus will eventually all but eradicate this "right."

Pro-abortion constitutional scholars sheepishly and understandably defend only the result of *Roe*. Further, all who support *Roe* as a matter of constitutional jurisprudence must do so only by viewing the Constitution as "living and breathing." In other words, the inanimate Constitution "lives" or changes to fit the views of those who would not afford the same right to the unborn. Abortion rights as a matter of constitutional law cannot be defended in an intellectually honest manner. Let's face it: Abortion rights advocates didn't like what the Constitution said. So, they ignored the Constitution and said it "breathes" or changes to suit their legislative predilections. *Roe* is the Dred Scott of the 20th century; it amounts to systemic suicide in which the judicial branch unconstitutionally seized power from the legislative branch. As such, *Roe* has spawned all manner of legal and political problems. For one thing, it stands the legal system on its head.

Should the innocent get the benefit of the doubt?

Our legal system is predicated upon granting the benefit of the doubt to those accused of a crime. Indeed, those who face the death penalty are given, in fact, every possible chance and benefit of the doubt. This is as it should be. That is, we want to do our best to ensure that we don't condemn an innocent person to death. So, we on occasion err on the side of the guilty to protect that one potential innocent person. In the case of the unborn, you and I must admit that we honestly can't say exactly how God views that little being. As previously stated, I have my thoughts. You have yours. But since we don't know on this side of heaven, innocent life should always get the benefit of the doubt. Why do we give criminals the benefit of the doubt but not the unborn? How can a criminal's rights be treated as sacred when life is not?

Roe has poisoned American politics.

Through *Roe*, the Supreme Court has injected a poison pill into American politics that cannot be digested. In *Roe*, the Court nationalized its view of abortion rights. As a result, Texas and California were decreed to, a practical matter, view this issue the same. New York and Georgia were declared ideological clones. This is the practical result. As we know, however, the nation has diverse and strongly-held views on this subject. Abortion is a 50-50 issue. It is certainly no more a violation of conscience for a woman to be unable to have an abortion in a particular state than for the residents of a state to be forbidden from protecting innocent life. The question is: Whose conscience is being violated? As a result of the abortion pill being put in the stew of American politics, each presidential election features a debate (albeit generally shallow) on the subject. The issue is part of each presidential election and the partisans all line up on their respective sides, but nothing changes because the Supreme Court does not change.

Abortion has led to the politicization of the judiciary

The judicial branch of the federal government was intended to be exempt from political pressures. Hence, federal judges are not subject to elections and serve for life. Now, with abortion and the potential review/limitation of *Roe*, each judicial nominee is subjected to a rigorous screening process that in fact focuses on one central issue: Is that judge pro-life? This is wrong, but this what the systemic suicide of *Roe* has wrought. So, now we must ask: Can a practicing Catholic judge be confirmed to the federal bench? If not, why then can a Unitarian be confirmed? Or a liberal Methodist?

So bad is the political polarization that the Democrats will not even let a pro-lifer speak at their national convention. Republicans at least tolerate different viewpoints on the issue. Yet, the truth is that a pro-abortion rights Republican cannot make it through the primaries. Of course, if abortion rights hadn't been declared sacred by the Supreme Court, the political parties would be free to address issues such as national security, economics, and the like. This is how our founders envisioned the national political debate. Smart men, they were. A national debate on morality and religion every four years will drive a nation to drink, so to speak.

The social infrastructure is in place to help women and welcome the unborn

Virtually everyone agrees that abortions should be "rare." At least that's what people say. If so, then no one should object as we try to limit the number of abortions. Adoption is a real option that offers hope to the birth mother and the adoptive parents. The truth is that there are very few, truly "unwanted" children. Untold thousands of couples wait for many months to adopt a child.

Also, crisis pregnancy centers are flourishing, providing real help and support in a non-judgmental environment. For many years, abortion-rights advocates said that women with unwanted pregnancies had no options. This criticism has led the pro-life community to respond. This is critical, because most women have abortions because they think their lives will essentially be over if they have an unwanted child without the means of supporting the child. We in the pro-life movement do such women a disservice by preaching to them about the sanctity of life. The best thing for such women is to provide them with the hope of options and help in the case of an unwanted pregnancy. That is, women need to be shown that there is hope for their lives and there are options other than abortion. This has happened on a massive scale as crisis pregnancy centers are now available in virtually every area of the country.

Abortion rights advocates have effectively conceded this debate.

People who argue exceptions (i.e., "back alley abortions" and rape/incest) to make a rule are in trouble in a debate. And any time someone comes up with an excuse to take a subject off the table completely, you know their argument is in real trouble. As mentioned above, almost all abortion rights advocates have conceded that abortions should be "rare." Abortions are not a good thing. Why? Well, our conscience tells us that abortions should be rare because they end an innocent life and alter another one forever.

Some people want the opportunity to continue the practice. I want the opportunity to at least be heard on limiting it. We should at least be able to have the debate. How can abortion rights be sacred if life is not?

4 November 2005

On Alito … For the life of 'em, the MSM just can't get it

The Christian Science-Monitor [recently] gushed that "3 out of 4 Alito rulings favored abortion rights." This is sloppy, misleading reporting. To be fair, three of the four Alito opinions dealing with abortion did not restrict abortion rights, either.

But the opinions do provide a key insight into the philosophy of Judge Alito. It is a philosophy that I, as a judicial conservative and *Roe* critic, am very comfortable with. The bottom line: I thought that

Alito was a superb choice when he was announced. My review of his abortion-related decisions makes me even more convinced of my initial impression. ...

So, here they are, in chronological order:

Planned Parenthood v. Casey (1991)

Judge Alito's dissenting opinion in this case has by far garnered the most attention of any of his opinions to date. Most have focused on the result, where Judge Alito voted to uphold Pennsylvania's spousal notification provision. Yet, the SC ultimately and narrowly disagreed with Judge Alito's powerfully persuasive opinion. More importantly, the *Casey* dissent now provides valuable insight as to just what kind of legal reasoning he will bring to the SC.

Here is his dissent, in a nutshell:

> "I do not believe that [spousal notification] has been shown to impose an undue burden as that term is used in the relevant Supreme Court opinions; I therefore apply the second prong of the two-part test; and I conclude that [spousal notification] is constitutional because it is 'rationally related' to a 'legitimate' state interest."

In *Casey*, Judge Alito examined the "undue burden" test, as enunciated by the architect of the test, Justice Sandra Day O'Connor. He persuasively demonstrated that spousal notification did not run afoul of this test by comfortably citing a litany of precedents (mostly authored by O'Connor herself) to undermine the majority's conclusion. ...

Of critical importance to Judge Alito, the notice provision at issue in *Casey* contained four exceptions. That is, a woman would not be required to notify her husband if she certified that she believed that: "(1) he is not the father of the child, (2) he cannot be found after diligent effort, (3) the pregnancy is the result of a spousal sexual assault that has been reported to the authorities, or (4) she has reason to believe that notification is likely to result in the infliction of bodily injury upon her." Absent the application of one of these exceptions, failure to make the required notice was a third-degree misdemeanor.

Planned Parenthood offered expert testimony that most battered women would be psychologically incapable of taking advantage of the fourth exception, that is, the exception for cases in which the woman has reason to fear that notification will lead to the infliction of bodily harm upon her. In response to this facially reasonable argument, however, Judge Alito showed a reluctance to accept the arguments supporting an expansive view of abortion rights. Specifically, Judge Alito seemed unwilling to accept the argument that abortion rights should remain constitutionally unfettered because of the potential for women to be victimized by abusive relationships when an unwanted pregnancy is involved:

> The plaintiffs failed to show how many ... married women seeking abortions without notifying their husbands are victims of battering. Thus, the opinion offered by their expert, even if taken at face value, merely describes the likely behavior of most of the women in a group of unknown size. Clearly then, this evidence does not show how many women would be inhibited or otherwise harmed by [the spousal notification provision]. I cannot believe that a state statute may be held facially unconstitutional simply because one expert testifies that in her opinion the provision would harm a completely unknown number of women.

However, the judge then acknowledged the seriousness of women's plight when confronted with an unwanted pregnancy in a difficult marriage. Yet, Judge Alito steadfastly acknowledged the limited role of the courts in such situations:

> Needless to say, the plight of any women, no matter how few, who may suffer physical abuse or other harm as a result of this provision is a matter of grave concern. It is apparent that the Pennsylvania legislature considered this problem

and attempted to prevent [the spousal notice provision] from causing adverse effects by adopting the four exceptions noted above. *Whether the legislature's approach represents sound public policy is not a question for us to decide. Our task here is simply to decide whether [the spousal notice provision] meets constitutional standards.* The first step in this analysis is to determine whether [the spousal notice provision] has been shown to create an undue burden under Supreme Court precedent, and for the reasons just explained it seems clear that an undue burden has not been established. (emphasis added)

Judge Alito then went into a somewhat extended discussion of the rational basis test. In this discussion, he frontally assaulted feminist dogma by laying out a father's interest in the life of his unborn child. He cited a number of Supreme Court precedents to support this proposition, too. He concludes with the following quote from a dissenting opinion of Justice White: "A father's interest in having a child—perhaps his only child—may be unmatched by any other interest in his life."

Finally, Judge Alito then laid out his rationale for upholding the spousal notice provision while reiterating his role in this dispute:

The Pennsylvania legislature could have rationally believed that some married women are initially inclined to obtain an abortion without their husbands' knowledge because of perceived problems—such as economic constraints, future plans, or the husbands' previously expressed opposition— that may be obviated by discussion prior to the abortion. In addition, the legislature could have reasonably concluded that [the notice provision] would lead to such discussion and thereby properly further a husband's interests in the fetus in a sufficient percentage of the affected cases to justify enactment of this measure. Although the plaintiffs and supporting amici argue that [the notice provision] will do little if any good and will produce appreciable adverse effects, the Pennsylvania legislature presumably decided that the law on balance would be beneficial. *We have no authority to overrule that legislative judgment even if we deem it "unwise" or worse.* (emphasis added)

What we see here is a judge, who though apparently is not a fan of abortion rights, clearly has a respect for the rule of law and precedent, and he further understands the role of the courts and legislatures in our system of government. In my view, his *Casey* dissent shows that he will be a judge who will not seek results that comport with his pro-life philosophy. Yet, I expect his persuasive, logical argumentation and commitment to the proper role of judges to erode *Roe* … over time.

Blackwell Health Center for Women v. Knoll (1995)

Judge Alito did not write this opinion, but he did join in the majority opinion. The result of the *Blackwell* opinion was that Medicaid funding was required, per federal regulations, for abortions as a result of rape and incest. This is about as far as many look at this opinion. Yet, there is quite a bit more to it.

Most importantly, the case was not about the constitutionality or propriety of abortions. Rather, the case was about the interpretation of administrative law. Bored yet? Sit tight. For a great overview of the case, Ed Whelan explains:

> The threshold question of administrative law that divided the majority and the dissent was the question of whether principles of so-called Chevron deference applied to the HHS action or whether instead so-called Skidmore deference applied. This question, which routinely arose in lots of cases involving review of administrative

action, was unsettled at the time, both in the Third Circuit and elsewhere. Justice Scalia has been the most vigorous advocate of an expansive realm for Chevron deference, but his views lost out in the 2001 decision in *United States v. Mead,* which, in Scalia's words, made "an avulsive change in judicial review of federal administrative action" by cutting back the realm of cases where Chevron deference applies. ...

Then, Whelan reminds conservatives of why this case should make them happy, and conversely why this case should disturb liberals:

In sum, while this case obviously arose in a context involving abortion, the question that divided the majority and the dissent was a general threshold question of administrative law on which *Alito was exactly where Scalia was.* There is no basis for inferring from this case anything about how Alito would approach other cases involving abortion—other than that Alito would apply the law neutrally and not indulge his own policy preferences (whatever they might be). That is exactly what everyone should want in a Supreme Court justice. ... (emphasis added.)

Thus, to the uninformed observer, this case makes it appear as if Judge Alito favors federal funding of abortions, or he "ruled in favor of abortion rights." Yet, the case actually provides evidence of similarities between Scalia and Alito on an important issue —their dislike of excessive judicial review of legislative and administrative actions.

Alexander v. Whitman (1997)

This is my favorite of the four. It seems completely misunderstood and the significance of Judge Alito's brief but profound concurring opinion could be enormous, in my view. In this case, Judge Alito agreed with the majority that injury to a stillborn child was not recognized in New Jersey as cause of action. Yet, he concurred to emphasize two points that are germane to this case and also any future analysis of *Roe* or other cases involving the expansion of new-fangled constitutional rights via the concept of "substantive due process" flowing from the 14th Amendment. Here is Judge Alito's opinion in its entirety:

> I am in almost complete agreement with the court's opinion, but I write to comment briefly on two points. First, I think that the court's suggestion that there could be "human beings" who are not "constitutional persons" is unfortunate. I agree with the essential point that the court is making: that the Supreme Court has held that a fetus is not a "person" within the meaning of the Fourteenth Amendment. However, the reference to constitutional non–persons, taken out of context, is capable of misuse. Second, I think that our substantive due process inquiry must be informed by history. It is therefore significant that *at the time of the adoption of the Fourteenth Amendment and for many years thereafter, the right to recover for injury to a stillborn child was not recognized.* (emphasis added).

Some may not realize it, but underlying Judge Alito's opinion is likely a healthy, conservative skepticism for new civil causes of action and the ambulance chasers who hawk them.

More importantly, though, this brief opinion establishes two things about Judge Alito's constitutional philosophy that are quite important: First, he objects to failing to afford constitutional rights to any human being. This perhaps allows for the potential of granting constitutional rights to the unborn as medical science advances. Second, and even more importantly, though, Judge Alito interprets the 14th Amendment in light of what it meant to the American people at the time of its adoption. For those who don't realize the significance of this view, recall that judges in the last 30 years have found all sorts of rights (abortion, sodomy, etc.) emanating from the 14th Amendment. How these rights were there all along and escaped the sharp legal eyes of the SC jurists of yore is beyond me. … How many states thought of abortion or any other new-fangled "rights" such as gay marriage as "fundamental rights" when the 14th Amendment was ratified after the Civil War?

Planned Parenthood v. Farmer (2000)

The MSM simplistically reports Judge Alito's opinion in this case as "striking down New Jersey's partial birth abortion law." It is true that Judge Alito concurred in the Third Circuit's opinion that did just that. But the existence of a concurring opinion should be a tip-off; there is more than meets the eye. In fact, I think there is significantly more. Orin Kerr had an excellent post on the Farmer decision.

Kerr explains the procedural background:

> Farmer involved a challenge by Planned Parenthood to a 1997 New Jersey statute that prohibited what is popularly known as the "partial birth abortion" procedure. A panel of the Third Circuit consisting of Judges Barry, Garth, and Alito heard argument in the case in November 1999. On January 14, 2000, while the panel was drafting its majority opinion, the Supreme court granted certiorari in a Nebraska case raising the same issue. The Third Circuit panel held its drafted opinion until the Supreme Court decided the Nebraska case on June 26, 2000. Instead of rewriting the panel opinion along the lines of the Supreme Court's new decision, *Stenberg v. Carhart,* Judge Barry simply added a new introductory paragraph to the opinion that she had drafted before the Supreme Court's decision and published her opinion otherwise "as is." The first paragraph of Judge Barry's opinion explains what happened:

'The majority opinion which follows was in final form before the Supreme Court of the United States heard argument in the appeal of *Carhart v. Stenberg*, 192 F.3d 1142 (8th Cir.1999). The Supreme Court has now issued its opinion in that case, finding Nebraska's "partial birth abortion" statute—a statute nearly identical to the one before this Court—unconstitutional. See *Stenberg v. Carhart*, 530 U.S. 914, 120 S.Ct. 2597, 147 L.Ed.2d 743 (2000). Because nothing in that opinion is at odds with this Court's opinion; because, in many respects, that opinion confirms and supports this Court's conclusions and, in other respects, goes both further than and not as far as, this opinion; and, because we see no reason for further delay, we issue this opinion without change.'

Judge Alito did not join in Judge Barry's opinion. Instead, he concurred, and in what appears to be an angry (in judicial terms, at least, and especially for Judge Alito) opinion, he chastised Barry for her majority opinion:

'I do not join Judge Barry's opinion, which was never necessary and is now obsolete. That opinion fails to discuss the one authority that dictates the result in this appeal, namely, the Supreme Court's decision in *Stenberg v. Carhart*, 530 U.S. 914, 120 S.Ct. 2597, 147 L.Ed.2d 743 (2000). Our responsibility as a lower court is to follow and apply controlling Supreme Court precedent.' ...

So, why the angst by Judge Alito in this case? First, this case again shows his penchant for addressing only the issues necessary for deciding a particular case; he clearly felt the majority was out of bounds in issuing its own opinion while the Supreme Court was considering *Stenberg*, which would control the outcome of the case.

More fundamentally, though, I think that Judge Alito was perturbed because he was not in the majority in the original (never issued) opinion. The issuance of such an opinion would have forced him to dissent in this case, and thus unnecessarily go on the record —again —against abortion rights in a high-profile case.

Query: Can you name a SC nominee who has issued two high-profile opinions advocating the limitation of abortion rights? I didn't think so.

Instead, Judge Alito issued a concurring opinion in which he followed SC precedent in striking down New Jersey's partial-birth abortion law. And the MSM, in my judgment, continues to miss the whole point.

But I am fairly sure that I don't. And the point is: Conservatives have little to fear from SC-Justice-to-be Sam Alito. But the Left? They should be greatly afraid.

Note: And recent history now shows that I was right about both Harriet Miers and her very able replacement pick, Justice Sam Alito.

19 September 2005

The Real Ken Starr

This past weekend, I had the privilege of emceeing a fundraising banquet for a local group that assists young women encountering crisis pregnancies ... both before and after. And the assistance, although given from a pro-life perspective, is offered to all regardless of their choice. It was indeed a moving evening.

The keynote speaker was Judge Ken Starr. He remarks were fabulous. But the man himself is more impressive.

Here is my intro of the judge:

"Our speaker this evening is from Vernon, Texas, where he was born in 1946. After graduation from Duke law school, Judge Starr went on to clerk for Chief Justice Warren Burger. Later, he served on the D.C. Circuit Court of Appeals, widely regarded as the second most powerful court in the land, as well as a prime launching pad for future Supreme

Court justices. Then, in 1989 the first Pres. Bush asked Judge Starr to be the U.S. Solicitor General. The S.G. is the nation's advocate before the Supreme Court, and it is regarded as the top practicing lawyer job in the nation.

"This career path may sound familiar. In fact, it sounds a lot like that of soon-to-be Chief Justice John Roberts. Indeed, Judge Roberts worked for Judge Starr at the Solicitor General's office. So, the heir-apparent as our next chief justice once called Judge Starr, our speaker tonight … 'boss.'

"What most people know about Judge Starr, though, is his most famous job, which was, of course, his service as Independent Counsel for 5 years during the Clinton Administration. Life is funny that way. Sometimes we are quote "known" and defined by things that really do not tell the whole story. For the truth is that, but for Judge Starr's most famous assignment, he would certainly be on a short list to have a job with much more notoriety … as a justice on the U.S. Supreme Court. He is clearly one of our nation's preeminent legal minds.

"Since 2004, Judge Starr has served as the dean of Pepperdine University Law School … suffering for Jesus in Malibu, California.

"Judge, I wanted to interview some witnesses … at least one … at Pepperdine to find out about the real you. So, I spoke with Ryan, your assistant, and she gave me the low down.

"Judge Starr likes to sing, like in the office sing. She told me about a trip she was taking to Chicago, and this apparently brought on an impromptu serenade involving some Chicago song by Sinatra? She says the judge is pretty good, too.

"But more importantly, I wanted to know what kind of man and boss he is. She expressed regret that she had not worked for the judge longer, and simply said, 'He is a wonderful man.' She went on to say that he is revered and respected by all who work with him and for him. He treats everyone with dignity and respect.

"This is I already knew, but I went to get the evidence to present to you. So, it is now my privilege to introduce to you … a great lawyer, a great American, a great man … Judge Ken Starr."

I watched the judge interact with people throughout the evening. I watched him patiently pose for pictures, answer questions, take time with each person. He makes each person around feel like they have dignity. Because they do to Judge Starr. Each person is worthy of dignity and respect. Oh, that all judges would behave that way. ...

21 October 2005

The Evil that is a Political Prosecution

... [Former House Majority Leader, Republican Tom] Delay has an interesting strategy: Taking on political adversaries head on and winning. Thus, he faces his current political prosecution. He will beat the rap, though. Know why? There's no "rap" to beat, as his "crime" is understood only in the minds of ... the most partisan of partisans. I mean, what did he do? He reversed what the Demos had been doing in Texas for 100 years and help land additional Republican congressional seats. Oh?

Meanwhile, in Washington, the Bush Administration awaits word of whether indictments will be issued against Karl Rove and Scooter Libby in yet another political "crime." But ... I thought if we made nice with the Left that they would make nice and not try to destroy us? Well, Virginia, there is a Hard Left, and they will never forgive Pres. Bush for not being one of them and daring to successfully use military force against the enemies of civilization.

All of you Demos/Hard Lefties that are cheering these political prosecutions might take a deep breath and ask if you really think a free society can afford to go this way. The guy in the over-size crib in the Baghdad courtroom used to go after political opponents by utilizing the "scales of justice."

This is where such deplorable tactics ultimately take us.

Free societies don't criminalize political opposition. For long, that is.

This is why you need judges committed to a consistent application of the governing law. This is why a judge's commitment to a faithful interpretation of what the text says is more important than a judge's predilections ...

Note: Speaking of "deplorable" tactics, the Head Deplorable has found himself in the crosshairs of his own political prosecution, indeed, an investigation in search of a crime and apparently for political purposes. This problem is a big a threat as ever, and it is time for Special Counsels to go the way of the buffalo.

28 October 2005

The Evil that is a Political Prosecution (Cont.)

… In my view, [political prosecutions] are dangerous legal/quasi-political animals. They may eat up your political adversary today, but tomorrow they will eat us all up.

So, what do I mean by "political" prosecution? First, it is a criminal action. As such, the power of the state is arrayed against the individual defendant. Second, these prosecutions are usually not for, or related to, crimes recognized at common law, such as burglary, sexual assault, murder, etc. In other words, the crimes are created by statute and interestingly are often not readily identifiable as crimes by ordinary people (As an example, ask some guy on the street what is the evil that Tom Delay is accused of doing). Third, political prosecutions occur as a result of a complaint by a political opponent seeking a political advantage via the proceedings.

Tomorrow, Scooter Libby, the VP's Chief of Staff, apparently will be indicted. I agree with Michael Barone that an indictment of either Libby or Karl Rove in the Plame matter would be a "grave injustice."

Let me explain. In '02-'03, certain elements within the CIA were fighting their own war with the White House. This was, in fact, a political war, with the two sides having different views about the desirability of taking out Saddam. In spite of the chain of command and their roles as public servants, however, Democrat Joseph Wilson and his Democrat wife were aiding the CIA forces in rebelling against WH policy. The punch line here in this whole mess is that Joseph Wilson is a lying, political hack who was, in the course of his political dispute with the WH, caught in the act of lying and hacking. Barone writes:

True, Rove and Libby did seek to discredit Joseph Wilson —as they should well have done. As the Senate Intelligence Committee concluded in a bipartisan report in July 2004, just about everything Wilson said publicly about his trip to Niger was untrue. He said that he had discredited reports that Iraq sought to buy uranium in Niger. But the CIA people to whom he reported concluded that, if anything, he substantiated such reports. He said that he pointed out that certain other intelligence reports were forged. But the forgeries did not appear until eight months after his trip. He said his wife had nothing to do with his trip to Niger. But it was she who recommended him for the trip. And on and on.

So, after Rove and Libby sought to set the record straight, Wilson and his political allies sought to cast these actions as criminal, intimating that Plame's life had been endangered. This is garbage. As Barone points out, for a variety of reasons it has become apparent that an indictment for the crime of "outing" Plame appears untenable. Thus, Libby is apparently to be charged only with his failure to be honest with the grand jury during the special prosecutor's probe.

Let's get some preliminaries out of the way. Should one lie to a grand jury? Of course not. It's wrong and it undermines the investigatory process. End of story. But should one be criminally prosecuted —and potentially face jail time and the loss of a career —for it? Well, it depends. Yes, it depends.

If one is lying to cover up a real crime, then yes, in my judgment a perjury/false statement indictment is within a prosecutor's discretion. If, however, one is lying to cover up ... well, something that shouldn't have been investigated in the first place, i.e., the prosecutor has no grounds to pursue an indictment for an underlying crime, then no ... absolutely not.

Perhaps a further, albeit imperfect, illustration is in order. Imagine you are sleeping soundly in your bed and then two guys break in, shine a flash light in your eyes and start questioning you about your whereabouts the night before. Realizing that you were out late at a place/with a person/in a situation where you should not have been, you lie. You lie big. Well, it turns out that there was a murder committed last night. You didn't commit it, but you are charged with making a false statement to a police officer, though. Too bad. And, oh yeah, your angry neighbor told the authorities to check you out. And by the way, your neighbor's friend actually committed the murder. But you committed an offense. Rules is rules. Feel good about that prosecution? You get the picture.

There are so very many things that are technically offenses (maybe this is what Sen. Hutchinson was referring to in her inartful remarks about perjury being a "technicality") but in reality no harm is done to the public, and thus a prosecutor accordingly should not proceed. Indeed, this happens every day. It is called prosecutorial discretion. The rules of ethics governing criminal prosecutors require a prosecutor to seek justice, not simply a conviction.

The bottom line: It is grossly unfair to criminally prosecute someone for "covering up" something that was not, in fact, a crime. This is especially so when such a prosecution is initiated by political enemies of the defendant and no harm has been suffered.

In such a case, the government, instead of representing the people, really prosecutes the people.

14 April 2007

R.I.P. Americans' Ability to Think

It's official. It's over. It's gone.

We can't think any more, as the Duke lacrosse case demonstrates [three members of the Duke University lacrosse team were falsely accused of rape in 2006 even though they were convicted in the court of public opinion by an overzealous prosecutor]. And our character (though perhaps not to the level of Europistan) is faltering. It's a deadly combination. Thinking is a moral exercise, in large part ... I think.

I've followed the Duke case, but not as close as many. I followed it closely enough to know that the charges should have been dropped long ago. As a former prosecutor, I take serious the prosecutor's oath not only to seek a conviction, but also justice. That is, a prosecutor is not ethically permitted to try a defendant for a crime just to "check it out." In other words, the prosecutor must first be convinced that he is prosecuting a guilty party, and then that the evidence supports the charge.

We do this because a criminal charge in a free society is a serious thing. It's something separated from politics, or at least it's supposed to be. When criminal charges cease to be taken seriously and are instead viewed as political acts, then we've really got serious problems. And our freedom is in jeopardy.

You all know the details of the Duke case now. D.A. Mike Nifong ran crazy with a disjointed, confused case based on conflicting stories, a constitutionally-improper line-up, and no DNA ... no wait, with DNA that contradicted the accuser's claims. The accuser, by all accounts, was entirely without credibility and very troubled.

But Nifong apparently ran with this case and filed charges to solidify the black vote in Durham as his Democratic Primary approached. Initially, based upon the first impressions and prejudices of the MSM/Demo/Left/Same Thing set, the case was off and running, with or without evidence.

Thankfully, the wheels eventually came off. Our system still works, in large part, because of two things: 1) We have a large number of checks and balances, such as appellate courts, civil courts, the legislative branch, and even the bar itself; and 2) ultimately, there are still good people around who take pride in their oaths as officers of the court.

I know, I like the lawyer jokes, too. But lawyers ultimately stopped this case.

Still, I think the Nifong matter is an extremely troubling example of the dangerous trend of increasing political prosecutions that must not only be stopped but reversed.

More and more, we have seen the criminal justice system used as a political tool. Libby and Delay are two recent examples that come to mind, but there are many others. Once upon a time, they did the same thing to Kay Bailey Hutchison around these parts [Republican Sen. Hutchison was ultimately acquitted in 1994 of misusing her office of State Treasurer in a case brought by Travis County Democrat D.A. Ronnie Earle]. And now, we see the Demos threaten to turn the routine firing of U.S. attorneys into a crime. Perjury traps are not only set, they are sprung, cases are tried, and lives ruined. Political "dirty tricks" are now "crimes."

So, Michael Jackson and O.J. Simpson are free, but Scooter Libby is a criminal? Martha Stewart, whom I am no fan of, is nailed for the vicious act of what? Help me out here. It's the world upside-down.

Have we gotten so morally upright that we have less tolerance for all manner of wrong-doing? Quite the contrary, I think we've degraded ourselves to the point where we can't tell the difference between ill-advised or bad conduct and a crime against society.

But it goes deeper than that. We now think that a finding of "Not Guilty" is a finding of "Virtuousness." No wait, many don't know what "virtuous" means. We think "Not Guilty" means "Good Guy." This is what happens when the clearly-marked lines between criminal and non-criminal conduct are erased and then moved ... and erased again, as needed.

Back to the Duke case, this means that the lacrosse players are now "Good Guys." Being falsely accused and subjected to an unfair media onslaught as they were, they are not only Good Guys, but bona fide Heroes to us now.

To put a cherry on top, they are now even concerned about "the little guy" who may not have the means to fight off a political prosecution. Pass the tissue. Really? I'm sorry, but call me skeptical about these claims which sound a bit scripted to me. Maybe they do feel this way, but these were no choir boys. After all, it was a stripper party we had there. And one of the lads has a conviction in another assault. I am just not getting images of Mom and apple pie with these guys. In fact, they might even be spoiled little punks. Maybe they were then but are not now. We don't know.

It takes some thought, some analysis. It takes more than five minutes. Life is simple of many levels but complicated on many, as well. We see this in the Duke case.

Being "not guilty" means you aren't guilty of this charge or it can't be proven beyond a reasonable doubt. It doesn't make you a hero.

But to the thoughtless generation, it does.

So now ... Political prosecutions are still permitted, and the accused Duke lacrosse players are heros.

But at least Mike Nifong may be on his way to being a Not Good Guy. ...

DC Shutdown: And now, in the Trump Administration, another special prosecutor makes his case while making mine again. Perhaps ironically, Trump pardoned Scooter Libby, the old Bush hand. Though perhaps none but his most deplorable supporters could have foreseen it, Pres. Trump's position in pushing back against the application of the law as an instrument of political power—both via judicial nominations and fighting political prosecutions (including his own)—has completely vindicated conservatives who voted for him on this basis. In the next chapter, I turn to the centrality and value of military service to those who love America and support its current commander-in-chief.

Chapter Seven

Just a U.S. Marine, but Plenty Enough

6 June 2005
Do you know what today is?

My dad used to always ask me this familiar question on days like today. Thus, I didn't need a school teacher to remind me. I knew.

As the years have gone by, I have grown more and more in awe of the heroism of those who have gone before in the defense of freedom. On this day 61 years ago, young Americans and our allies stormed the beaches of Normandy to defeat the evil that was Hitler's Germany.

The most daring task in this most daring mission fell to the Army Rangers —specifically Lt. Col. James Earl Rudder's Second Ranger Battalion at a place called Pont-du-Hoc (pictured above-right). The task was straight-forward enough: Scale the 115'-125' cliffs under heavy German fire with approximately 300 men to take the position used for six huge 155mm guns, each with a range of fifteen miles. Thus, the success of the Rangers was vital to the overall success of the D-Day invasion.

Lt. Col. Rudder, a school teacher and football coach from Eden, Texas, personally led the assault. Nearly half of his Rangers were killed or wounded in ascending the cliffs.

But their courage —both moral and physical —was too much for the Nazi defenders. As fire rained down on the Americans, they looked evil in the eye and advanced. Evil blinked.

Hell has no fury like that of good men. The Rangers took the guns.

When their initial ascent had been successfully completed, Lt. Col. Rudder's communications officer sent the signal: "Praise the Lord."

Note: The foregoing little post was cited by Instapundit, giving me my first and only Insta-launch.

27 May 2005
Memorial Day Address

The following are my Memorial Day remarks delivered on Sunday, May 29, 2005:

This morning as we look out from the front porches of our homes in the land that Pres. Reagan called the "Shining City on a Hill," we remember what it has cost to build and defend this land. We remember all the members of our military who have paid for our freedom with their lives.

I would like to provide you a snapshot of one particular sacrifice by one American defending a hill in a faraway land. Perhaps it will encourage you (as it has me) to remember the sacrifices of those who have made our freedom possible.

In the Spring and Summer of 1990, I was a one of a class of a couple of hundred Marine lieutenants trying to find my way through The Basic School —a six-month-long indoctrination of Marine lieutenants learning the "basics" of leading an infantry platoon before being sent to our respective duty stations and jobs in the fleet.

TBS was grueling, boring, and high-stress-inducing all in one. Job selections and duty stations depended upon performance. And worse still, the Marine Corps looked for a few, maybe as many of a half-dozen of us, who might have slipped through the cracks at OCS —those lieutenants who either needed to be "recycled" through another TBS class or even worse ... discharged and sent home.

So, in addition to our concerns about our futures in the Corps, our fears of being one of those left behind drove us on. No one wanted to be at the bottom of the class.

Our land navigation class was an island of encouragement in a sea of exhaustion and dread. Each day a wiry, upbeat, square-jawed captain, whose name I still can't remember —to us, he was just "Capt. Land Nav" —would greet us with a wide, genuine smile and say, "It's a great day in the Marine Corps!! Hooyah!" Actually, the day usually wasn't good, but we would go wild anyway.

Then, before he would teach us land navigation, he would begin each day's class by reading a Medal of Honor Citation of a Marine. Day after day, we just sat in awe as Capt. Land Nav read us the citations of these heroes. Months of land navigation. Days, weeks, months of citations. We heard of the heroism of Marines in places like Belleau Wood, the Chosin Reservoir, Iwo Jima, and Vietnam. A number of these heroes were officers, too. Officers who had been there at TBS and tried to stay awake in classes, just like us. Every citation was amazing and inspiring. Yet, one stands out.

Here it is:

> BOBO, JOHN P.
> Rank and organization: Second Lieutenant, U.S. Marine Corps Reserve, 3d Battalion, 9th Marines, 3d Marine Division (Rein), FMF
> Place: Quang Tri Province, Republic of Vietnam
> Date: 30 March 1967
> Entered service at: Buffalo, New York
> Born: 14 February 1943, Niagara Falls, New York
> Citation: For conspicuous gallantry and intrepidity at the risk of his life above and beyond the call of duty.
>
> Company I was establishing night ambush sites when the command group was attacked by a reinforced North Vietnamese company supported by heavy automatic weapons and mortar fire. 2d Lt. Bobo immediately organized a hasty defense and moved from position to position encouraging the outnumbered Marines despite the murderous enemy fire. Recovering a rocket launcher from among the friendly casualties, he organized a new

launcher team and directed its fire into the enemy machine gun positions. When an exploding enemy mortar round severed 2d Lt. Bobo's right leg below the knee, he refused to be evacuated and insisted upon being placed in a firing position to cover the movement of the command group to a better location. With a web belt around his leg serving as a tourniquet and with his leg jammed into the dirt to contain the bleeding, he remained in this position and delivered devastating fire into the ranks of the enemy attempting to overrun the Marines. 2d Lt. Bobo was mortally wounded while firing his weapon into the main point of the enemy attack but his valiant spirit inspired his men to heroic efforts, and his tenacious stand enabled the command group to gain a protective position where it repulsed the enemy onslaught. 2d Lt Bobo's superb leadership, dauntless courage, and bold initiative reflected great credit upon himself and upheld the highest traditions of the Marine Corps and the U.S. Naval service. He gallantly gave his life for his country.

We sat in silent awe for a number of seconds.

And then Capt. Land Nav broke the silence: "There's more, lieutenants," he said. How could there possibly be more, we thought? There was no way.

"Lt. Bobo," the Captain said, "finished last in his class at The Basic School."

You could have heard a pin drop, as a couple hundred Marine lieutenants sat in stunned silence. All of us had been facing our fears for some time. All of us, whether we wanted to admit it or not, wondered: Would I have what it took not to let my fellow Marines down? Was I good enough?

And this guy ... this guy who had finished last ... truly, the last had become first. He had done more than any could have expected. He took his final stand defending the high ground on a faraway hill so that his comrades and the rest of us could live securely on the "high ground" at home.

I thought of Lt. Bobo for the rest of TBS. Remembering his sacrifice gave me confidence and courage.

Lt. Bobo's sacrifice dramatically impacted his comrades, too. These were men whom he literally and figuratively carried to the "high ground."

Fifteen Marines in Lt. Bobo's already-depleted platoon died on that fateful day in 1967. Nearly all of the survivors were wounded in the brutal onslaught of enemy mortar fire. But because of his sacrifice, Lt. Bobo helped 15 of his Marines not only to survive, but incredibly to repel the assault of an enemy with vastly superior numbers and firepower.

For the survivors, the 24-year-old lieutenant altered the course of their lives.

These were Marines with families. With children. With dreams. Like us. They told of Lt. Bobo's heroism, which had carried them back up the hill and home to the "Shining City."

One life willingly laid down became a pebble in the ocean of humanity. Which led to waves of inspiration ... of second-chances ... of victory ... of lives saved ... of dreams sustained ... of families reunited and children born ... of hope.

Some forget. They won't. They can't.

There are thousands and thousands of others who, like Lt. Bobo, have given all. Few know their stories. Perhaps none know. There is the soldier who fell on a grenade to save his friends. There is the pilot whose plane went down in the dark of night. There is the sailor at sea, doing his duty, when a boat full of terrorists rammed his ship with explosives. Each had a story. Each gave all they could give. Each carries us today.

When you're younger, it's hard to realize and appreciate what you have. It's hard to understand how blessed you are to wake up every day and already have the world by the tail simply because you are an American.

As you get older, though, you begin to realize that the good things in life are not accidents. Indeed, the really good things are the exceptions to the chaos and disappointment that often characterize this temporal world. The truly great things in this life don't just happen. They require great sacrifice.

Indeed, though the desire for it beats in every human heart, freedom is the exception in this world rather than the rule. Freedom does not spontaneously combust. Without those willing to make great sacrifice for freedom, yes to fight for it and even to die, we will ultimately have peace. But we will not have freedom.

But this can sometimes be hard to grasp when you are born in a "Shining City" ... indeed, on freedom's "hill."

Young people don't often feel the need to stop and reflect. They are moving too fast. Life calls. "Hurry!" it says. There is fun to be had, adventures to experience, boys and girls to meet, college degrees to attain, money to make, careers to plan.

But ironically freedom calls our young people back ... time and again ... to make the sacrifices continually required to reside on freedom's "hill." Because if you won't defend the hill you live on, ultimately you won't live there.

For tyranny does spontaneously combust. And then it advances on the free.

Approximately 1,800 young Americans have made the ultimate sacrifice in Afghanistan and Iraq since 9/11. They had dreams. They had comforts. They had opportunities. They had families.

They had children. About 1,300 children of service members have lost a parent (mostly fathers) since 9/11. This is sad, no doubt. However, we take comfort in knowing that these children have been left a legacy of service and dedication. And because of the example left to them —which they will remember —many of them will no doubt do the same.

Still more Americans will certainly perish in these conflicts we are fighting even as I speak. Why do they do it? They certainly didn't have to. In fact, they volunteered. They signed up because they love their country and their countrymen. They remembered what it takes to keep this land free.

"Greater love has no one than this, than to lay down one's life for his friends."

We remember.

21 February 2005

Who raises the flag of freedom when tyranny threatens?

John Bradley: Appleton, Wisconsin ...

Franklin Sousley: Hilltop, Kentucky ...

Harlon Block: Weslaco, Texas ...

Ira Hayes: Gila Indian Reservation, Arizona ...

Rene Gagnon: Manchester, New Hampshire ...

Mike Strank: Franklin Borough, Pennsylvania.

Most Americans don't know these names, but they know the picture of these six young men taken on February 23, 1945. On that date, Joe Rosenthal photographed these men raising the American flag on Mount Suribachi. This photo became the signature image of the U.S. Marines in the nation's most heroic battle —Iwo Jima.

Admiral Chester Nimitz aptly described the "uncommon valor" on Iwo that became a "common virtue." More Medals of Honor (27) were awarded in this battle than any other. More than 6,800 Americans died on Iwo Jima; most of them were Marines. Another 20,000 were wounded. Of the 22,000 Japanese defenders on Iwo, less than 1,000 survived. The battle lasted 35 days, more than a month after the famous photo. Indeed, most of the fighting and the casualties occurred after the the triumphant flag-raising. Half of the six flag-raisers would not leave the island alive.

Nearly five years ago, I read James Bradley's *Flags of our Fathers*, the story of the six Iwo Jima flag-raisers. This is a powerful book that I think every American should read. The stories of the six flag-raisers are a microcosm of the entire battle, the war in the Pacific, and indeed the great WWII generation that hoisted America on its back and led the nation to superpower status.

Flags of our Fathers makes it clear that we were fighting an enemy with a different view of human life than our own. The Japanese defenders of Iwo were ruthless and fanatical, and determined to fight to the death. Indeed, Bradley's book left me in awe of the sheer enormity of the dangers and horrors that the Marines encountered. Yet, the courage, fortitude, and astonishing character of the heroes of Iwo Jima is even more awe-inspiring than the daunting obstacles they faced.

Incidentally, the most decorated of the Iwo flag-raisers was not a Marine. He was a Navy corpsman, John "Doc" Bradley. He won the Navy Cross, second only to the Medal of Honor, for his actions on Iwo. Of the three flag-raisers who survived, Bradley was the only one to live a somewhat normal life after the war. (Ira Hayes' life was destroyed by alcohol. Rene Gagnon never adjusted to the fame that followed the three surviving flag-raisers.)

Still, Bradley was tormented by horrifying nightmares that left him crying in his sleep for years. Bradley was a private, quiet man, and his family did not know of his Navy Cross until after his death. …

Today's Marines are also facing a fanatical enemy who shows little regard for human life. Like their forebears, Marines in Iraq and Afghanistan are performing heroically. But today's Marines, like all of us, stand on the shoulders of the heroes of Iwo Jima. They showed the way.

It's important to recall, too, that when the Marines were hitting the beaches of Iwo Jima, the outcome of the war and America's place in the post-war world were not yet established. Now, though, because of their sacrifices and successes in securing beachheads in the cause of freedom, we look down and back and see how far they have carried us.

Semper Fidelis.

Note: In June 2016, a USMC investigation determined that—instead of John Bradley —PFC Harold Schultz of Los Angeles, CA raised the flag on Suribachi. Schultz quietly worked as a letter carrier for 30 years after returning from the Pacific.

10 November 2006

Here's to the "Old Corps"

Another year, another Marine Corps Birthday. As the years roll by, I am more grateful for having worn the Eagle, Globe, and Anchor.

Looking back, it was a crazy leap for me to sign up. What was I thinking? I had a cushy law job lined up at a big firm in Houston. But something was missing. I have talked before (last USMC Birthday, in fact) about the influence of my uncle. There was my dad, too, the squid who taught me to revere the Marines. I don't know. I just had to make the leap.

It's still the best professional decision I ever made. I can't even think of what is #2. It doesn't matter.

I will remind you again that I am no war hero. There are lots of new ones these days, in the USMC and our sister services. There are old ones who are still around, too. And I love every minute I get to interact with them. Heck, it's the best part of this blog gig for me. They all have my heartfelt thanks and deepest respect.

But I was just a Marine. That fact remains good enough for me.

The Corps stands on three pillars —dedication, brotherhood, and tradition.

I learned early and often that the Corps is about dedication to God, Country, and Corps. Marines are not ashamed of these things. They talk openly of their affection for their God, their nation, and the USMC that serves it. They are throwbacks.

And although they may get into fraternal scrapes, Marines love each other unashamedly. The greatest fear that every Marine lives with is that he may let down his brother Marines.

I remember [living] on base at Camp Pendleton. The sense of community at 216 Dolphin Drive is something that I cherish to this day. It was an amazing place where race, color, status, even faith didn't divide us. We were all just green anyway. We were Marines and Marine family members. We Marines went and did our jobs on the base. Some deployed. And when we were home, we watched each others' homes, each others' kids, and we supported each other as the Gulf War came and went.

One of my neighbors, a Cobra [helicopter] pilot, crashed and was killed near Kuwait after Desert Storm ended. He was one of the finest men I have known. He left behind a young wife and child. I was haunted by wondering how such great men could die so young. The Marines have seen a lot of this, though. A few months later, another neighbor who was a Huey pilot, was also killed. Our court on Dolphin Drive mourned together. Still we understood …

That's part of the tradition, the history. Once one is imbued with the rich history of the USMC, a near-magical force propels the new Marine to defend and guard that tradition, and to uphold it at all costs, and even build upon it.

I used to joke that the "Old Corps" began on the day before you signed up. But we all knew we rode on the shoulders of those who went before. They paved the way. They made the history. They earned the grudging respect of the Germans and the moniker "Devil Dog" in WWI. They landed on Guadalcanal when WWII was in doubt. They raised the flag on Iwo and died a few days later. They slogged away in Vietnam when much of the nation had forgotten what honor and duty were.

And tonight they will be patrolling and standing watch in Iraq … when many in the nation again ponder things that Marines never question.

So, here's to the new generation of Marines, who are riding on the shoulders of those in the "Old Corps" who went before. You are doing the nation proud.

But I'd like to dedicate this post to the "Old Corps," to those who went before … to those who answered the call when history was not yet made and when the country didn't appreciate your sacrifice. I will never forget. …

And I'd also like to thank those who love the Marine Corps and share the Marines' unrelenting commitment to the nation. Yes, this is the Marine Corps birthday, but the USMC belongs to America.

As I've said before, lots of nations have marines, but there is only one U.S. Marine Corps.

Semper Fidelis.

7 December 2006

7 December ... Remember how it started ... and ultimately ended

Days like these remind me of my old man. He never bought a Japanese car, and he chided me relentlessly when I bought even a used Toyota van years ago.

It's hard for many my age and younger to understand the shock and rage that was December 7, 1941.

But I was taught to remember. And so I always will.

Today is the 65th anniversary of the sneak attack on Pearl Harbor. Survivors, who have gotten together every five years since the attack, are dwindling. In fact, this year may be their final reunion.

Time and history march on. Indeed, the survivors of the "day that will live in infamy" are leaving us.

But we must not leave them.

The attack came on a Sunday morning, when the Japanese correctly assumed that our navy would be unprepared. But Japan could never have gotten a large enough head start on America to prevail in WWII. It still makes me shake my head, for totalitarians always mistake the outward manifestations of America's might for its soul.

Today, Japan is an ally and friend of the United States. That is a wonderful thing, and it is, in my view, a testimony both to the existence of God and to the greatness of the United States.

Anti-war protesters mark the anniversaries of the atomic bombings of Hiroshima and Nagasaki, but December 7 gets less press every year, it seems.

But I will always remember.

Indeed, we Americans need to remember how the nation got plunged into World War II. ...

And America's enemies would do well to remember how the war ended. I know some doubt that America can and will find the resolve to finish what tyrants have started. I think they are wrong.

America's totalitarian enemies continue to bet against history.

So, without criticizing those who like my dad who could not or cannot forgive, let me say that I have. ...

4 June 2007

Back to Quantico

Last week I made the trek back to Quantico for the first time since I got out of The Basic School (a six-month harassment package with the purported purpose of teaching new Marine lieutenants the basics of leading an infantry platoon) and high-tailed out of Dodge back in 1990. Most Marine lieutenants get the hyakah from Q-town and are not anxious to come back any time soon.

I was no different. So, it took me 17 years to get back.

But it was pretty special being back. I drove to Officer Candidates School, and I was shocked ... yes, shocked to find that it looked essentially identical to how I remembered it ... the obstacle courses, Brown Field (where we allegedly learned Close Order Drill), Bobo Hall (where I ate the only two helpings of liver that I have eaten in my life, and during the same meal), the squad-bays, the places where we hit the trails and the hills, etc. There were a few new buildings, but it was basically the same. Incredibly so.

I even recognized the trees ... the cedar trees that border Brown Field. Once, I tried to jam a shirt in one of them on the way out to the trails to run, only to get caught by the sergeant-instructor.

On the day of my return, new officer candidates were starting the whole process over. A new class was underway. I could tell by the hair (the presence thereof). Also, they were in formation outside the barber shop, which was, of course, where it has been since the dawn of time. Or so it seems. I could have walked right to it and gone straight to the chair. The barbers were always somewhat pleasant (relatively so).

It was a great day to be there, in this place of great challenges, laughs, anguish, and triumph.

Every Marine lieutenant who has been killed in Iraq earned his bars at this place.

Every Marine lieutenant who served in the first Gulf War became an officer here.

Every junior Marine officer since WWII was trained at Quantico.

All commissioned Marine officers who served in Vietnam got their start here ... like my uncle did.

Standing there on Brown Field, I sensed the presence of all of them. And it was humbling all over again to have the same title as they did and do —"Marine."

13 June 2005

D-Day Plus 7 … 61 Years Ago

He had just landed. In fact, he came ashore on Omaha Beach on 11 June 1944. He had the measles on D-Day. So, his landing on northern coast of France was delayed a bit.

He was one of the people I wanted to see this weekend, when for the first time in about 30 years, I went back to the family reunion … a place of good memories from my youth. He used to cook the barbecue at these events, but he has since given up those duties. My grandmother (his older sister) passed away nearly two years ago, and her passing set me on a course to reconnecting with my family roots. I meant to go last year but couldn't make it. This year, I'm glad I did.

He is a bit frailer now than he was as a 26-year-old staff sergeant. He has had some serious health struggles of late; in fact, he wasn't able to come to Houston see my grandmother as she battled heart disease two years ago.

But yesterday … there was my great-uncle, with a walker, a big cowboy hat, and a bigger smile. He was messing with everyone within earshot. He said I've "put on a little weight since he saw me last." He's right. I was about 12 then.

The family reunion was held in VFW Post #4006, in Navasota, Texas. As a life member of that post, my great-uncle enabled us to reserve the hall. He is one of the few surviving WWII members of Post #4006.

I went over and started picking his brain about his time in WWII. I had heard bits and pieces, but never from the man himself. He talked as a wise sage who says much less than he really saw and knows. He said he helped form a company from a group of soldiers who had spent time in the stockade; they were unruly, but they were tough and salty. He and these renegades arrived on Omaha Beach on D-Day + 5. They walked a full day or so ... and then for the next two months he encountered German soldiers on a near-daily basis as the Americans fought to liberate France, but mainly they just fought for their lives.

Many have not heard of the "Battle of the Hedgerows" in Northern France. It was a difficult and bloody stretch in the most difficult and bloody drive to liberate France. My great-uncle said he changed clothes once in a couple of months. He and his men pressed the attack while routinely facing desperate Nazis unleashing relentless machine gun and artillery fire. They spent weeks on end face-to-face with the enemy. In fact, they were often close enough to hear the enemy talking and screaming. But the Germans did much more than talk: "I didn't mind the machine guns so much," he said. "But the artillery ... it would come down and just scare you to death, but you couldn't move."

The big German guns rained down on 4 August 1944 near St. Lo, a town about 30 miles inland from the beaches of Normandy. The shelling was the most intense encountered thus far. His captain was decapitated by an artillery shell. My great-uncle himself then became a casualty as shrapnel from a shell ripped through his shoulder. He suffered a great loss of blood, and medics pleaded with him to hold on while he was taken to a field hospital, where he ended up spending three days. Then he was taken to a London hospital, where he stayed four months. Christmas was spent on a hospital ship crossing the Atlantic. When he returned home, he recuperated for many more months. But by the time he was finished recovering from his life-threatening injuries, the war was over ... won by his own sacrifices, as well as hundreds of thousands like him.

Like many others before and since, though, prevailing in combat really came down to just day-to-day survival. Taking care of your buddies. Making sure that you stayed awake while he slept, and vice-versa. Loving their country got them to the battlefield but loving each other would take them home.

He showed me his scar where they removed the pieces of the artillery shell. Still, they didn't get it all. His bride ... pulled pieces out for many months and even years, as the pieces would eventually come up to the skin where they could be removed.

Listening to him, I was reminded of how many think that the D-Day ended the German resistance in France and set the allies on a path directly to Berlin. Hardly. Bloody D-Day was only the beginning, and many, many Americans and other allied troops would die on the way to surgically removing the Nazi cancer from Europe. Then, Nazi "insurgents" or "werewolves" wreaked havoc even after the fall of … Germany. Thus, it remained a long road to defeating evil. …

11 November 2005

Calling All Vets …

Happy Veteran's Day. Man, what a week. Yesterday's post brought forth some of the best comments ever, and it led me to some other great posts and tributes. Some of you (and you know who you are) brought some tears to my eyes. And I thank you.

Today, we pause to remember the nation's veterans. In particular, my thoughts are with those who have fought in the nation's wars. It is good that we remember … and are reminded to remember. Have you noticed that people tend to forget what they should remember and vice versa? Funny.

But we should remember. Those who have been there and served, particularly those of you who have done so in wartime, have made this great American experiment a reality. For the longer we live, we see more and more evidence that the free are swimming upstream, and the enemies of freedom have many structural advantages and are constantly on the prowl. The enlightened among us have taught that as mankind advanced this would not be so. They have been proven wrong … over and over again.

What to make of this? To remain free, this nation will have to keep producing people who are willing to put it all on the line. So, how do we produce new generations of heroes? It starts in families. It continues with friends. It continues still with neighbors. And it continues on with even acquaintances.

Veterans should tell their stories. Tell people where you served and what you did. Tell them why you served. Tell your kids. Talk to your friends. Tell people about the moments that still make you cry. Live out who you are. Speak up when appropriate about the value, pride, and honor of wearing the uniform of the United States military.

We need to see. We need to hear. And for those who are doing it already, great. Keep on doing it. We need you.

Each vet has a story to tell. I know.

When I was seven, my family was in crisis. So, I went to Arizona to spend the summer with my uncle. He was a Vietnam vet, a Marine, a prior-enlisted company commander who did two tours. I later learned he also had two Bronze Stars and a Silver Star.

During that summer, my uncle used to wake me up early — usually with some saying about the value of getting up early and the vice of sleeping too much —to go out and feed the horses. He was chipper and cheerful, and he loved the Marine Corps. (Man, he still does, too.) He would read me snippets ... they often sounded strange and undiscernible at the time ... out of the Marine Corps Gazette. And then he would say, "What do you think of that, little buddy? The Marines are looking for good young men. Maybe you can grow up and be one someday." At times, I thought he was a bit corny, but I respected him. I knew that my uncle had a purpose much higher than himself and this affected me in ways I didn't fully understand at the time.

Later, when I when I was making the decision (a strange one, indeed, to my contemporaries) to go into the USMC, I recalled my uncle. His encouragement and example were big factors, along with the patriotism instilled in me by dad, that led me to sign up.

I never regretted it, and I wouldn't have missed it for anything. Actually, maybe I would have missed it but for the words and example of a vet.

DC Shutdown: History and necessity dictate the valuing of military service, and, for its part, the Trump Administration has signed into law one of the biggest defense spending increases in history while also emphasizing reform at the Veterans Administration. However, we who tend to trust our government on national security issues have had to learn the hard way that that the government's usage of our military in foreign lands without a clear national security interest has become all too common and must be opposed. It has been a process to come to realize this myself, and I suspect, for others, as well. The next chapter discusses the Iraq War, an unforgettable teaching tool in this regard.

Chapter Eight

The Iraq War

I was wrong about it before I was right about it.

9 February 2005

And now ... Gen. James Mattis's remarks to his Marines before the initial assault into Iraq in March 2003

For decades, Saddam Hussein has tortured, imprisoned, raped and murdered the Iraqi people; invaded neighboring countries without provocation; and threatened the world with weapons of mass destruction. The time has come to end his reign of terror. On your young shoulders rest the hopes of mankind.

When I give you the word, together we will cross the Line of Departure, close with those forces that choose to fight, and destroy them. Our fight is not with the Iraqi people, nor is it with members of the Iraqi army who choose to surrender. While we will move swiftly and aggressively against those who resist, we will treat all others with decency, demonstrating chivalry and soldierly compassion for people who have endured a lifetime under Saddam's oppression. Chemical attacks, treachery, and the use of the innocent as human shields can be expected, as can unethical tactics. Take it all in stride. Be the hunter, not the hunted: never allow your unit to be caught with its guard down. Use good judgment and act in the best interest of our Nation. You are part of the world's most feared and trusted force. Engage your brain before you engage your weapon. Share your courage with each other as we enter the uncertain terrain north of the Line of Departure. Keep faith with your comrades on your left and right and Marine Air overhead. Fight with a happy heart and strong spirit.

For the mission's sake, our country's sake, and the sake of the men who carried the Division's colors in past battles—who fought for life and never lost their nerve—carry out you mission and keep your honor clean. Demonstrate to the world that there is 'No Better Friend, No Worse Enemy' than a U.S. Marine.

J.N. Mattis
Major General, US Marines
Commanding

15 December 2005

"My case for the Iraq War ..."

You may recall that [fellow blogger] Jess invited me to debate with a former military type (an anti-war liberal) on issues surrounding the Iraq War and the War on Militant Islam. My worthy opponent has been out-of-pocket, however. I was thinking maybe his anti-war opinions would be posted on about Election Day. But ... who knows?

At any rate, here is my answer to Jess's Question #2:

On March 20, 2003, did I believe we were entering into a necessary conflict?

Absolutely. And I think it would have been irresponsible, in light of the evidence and the Saddam's history, to NOT take down Saddam's Iraq.

Less than a year-and-a-half after 9/11, we were still being run in circles by Saddam Hussein. Why wouldn't he allow weapons inspectors to do their jobs? The whole world had agreed for many years that he possessed weapons of mass destruction. At home, politicians of both American political parties agreed on this point. Again, this was a national consensus held for many years. In fact, I think this is why Pres. Clinton ostensibly sent in his air strikes in 1998, unless one believes he did it to deflect attention from his legal troubles.

But the analysis of war with Iraq involved and involves more fundamental changes in America's relationship to the world. In the wake of 9/11, America could not afford to wait for the next attack. The country would not permit it. Nor should the country permit it. The risks were and remain too great, and a saber-rattling dictator in the Middle East could not be tolerated. And we knew that Saddam not only would rattle the saber but that he would, from time to time, attack both his own people (with chemical weapons, no less) and his neighbors.

As should have been painfully obvious to all concerned, Militant Islamists had declared war on us as of the start of the Iraq War... actually, they had done so long prior to 9/11. Although the WH speaks in politically correct terms about the threat posed by Militant Islam, I think they realized what was going on. To say that there is no "operational connection" between Iraq and the jihadis who planned and carried out 9/11 is to miss the point. The point is: The conflict with Iraq arose in the context of a larger war with Militant Islam.

In my view, I think that most people who oppose the Iraq War either fail to understand the larger war with Militant Islamists or they are not on America's side in this war.

On Saddam's connections to terror, this we know: He harbored terrorists, i.e., Leon Klinghoffer's murderer, Ansar al-Islam, He paid for suicide bombers to attack Israel. He was a source of instability in the region for many years. (If you don't want to take my "word" for it, read a good liberal like Christopher Hitchens) And to say we should have dealt with him sooner is to say what? That the Clinton Administration was negligent? To say that we couldn't do more than had been done is to prove the ineffectiveness of the U.N., is it not?

Do I still support the war? Before getting to my answer, let me look at this question and describe a bit of my disappointment with the Bush Administration. What most people are asking when they ask this question is: Since we haven't found WMD and we have lost more than 2,000 troops, was it worth it? Well, like many, I was surprised that we didn't find more evidence of WMDs. We certainly found some, but not what virtually all (including the French and Russians) expected. I will note here, too, that the failure to find large stockpiles of WMD raises still other questions for me, such as: Since we know Saddam had them, where are they? And how could the world have been so wrong? How do we make sure our intelligence capabilities are what they need to be?

The Leftists who continue to argue that the Administration lied or manipulated intelligence are themselves lying. We know that, in fact, the PDBs [presidential daily briefings] that Pres. Bush was receiving painted an even darker picture in Iraq than the intelligence reports given to Congress. And the Brits incidentally still stand by their Niger report.

However, I do think the Bush Administration probably didn't fully anticipate all of the difficulties we would encounter in a post-Saddam Iraq. For sure, they failed to make the case early on —except in trite platitudes —regarding the difficulties ahead, and what was at stake in a stable Iraq that could defend itself from the jihadi threat. This is a great frustration for me, as I believe much can and should be said to rally public support in the larger struggle against Militant Islamists.

Here is my punch line, though: Taking down Saddam remains just as right today as it was on March 20, 2003. The world is better off, and we have seen the ripple effects in Lebanon, Libya, and throughout the region. To say America is making a positive difference in Iraq is hardly some fringe right-wing position, unless you consider people like Joe Lieberman, Christopher Hitchens, and Ed Koch to be fringe right-wingers. Whether democracy will ultimately work there remains to be seen, but it is important that the Iraqi government is not a source of instability and anti-American hatred.

Note, too, that Hillary is uncomfortable with what the Demo base is demanding —immediate withdrawal. How come? What does she know about the American public and the war that the Demo base fails to grasp?

Another important aspect to the war ... In Iraq we are delivering an important message to the jihadis in the country and elsewhere: We won't wait for you to come after us anymore. We will find you. We will do what we say we will do, including the dirty work of clearing jihadis house to house. It is hard to overstate the importance of confronting and proving wrong the jihadi template that Americans are soft, weak infidels. Let's face it, these are evil people we are fighting. And their ignorance of America and the modern world is breathtaking. The jihadis selectively recall the Somalia experience as an example of American vacillation and weakness. America has been shattering this template over the last three years.

On criticizing the war ... If I didn't support the war effort, I wouldn't be saying much about it. Why? It's hard to know the point. I mean, what is the idea? It looks to many people like the Left just wants to use the war as a vehicle for political gains, in particular to damage Pres. Bush. And to those who loudly argue that our troops' mission is based on a lie and is accomplishing no good purpose, what the hell is the purpose of such rhetoric? It sounds treasonous and it emboldens the enemy. And such arguments have a tangible, negative effect on our troops. This is why they overwhelmingly want the American people to be behind what they are doing, that is, to support their mission. Wars are won with young troops whose morale and esprit de corps are critical to their success. The time for debating whether we should be involved in military action in Iraq ended when the enemy started putting bullets down range. Sure, people have a right to speak. And I do, too. And I will remind them that their actions are increasing the likelihood that young Americans will get killed. Intentions are irrelevant here. Words and actions have consequences.

When you have to check to see if a statement was made by Kennedy or Zarqawi, you know we have a problem.

It seems funny to me, too, that people want to elevate the opinions of former military types like Murtha, Kerry, and McCain to "super opinion" status, but they won't listen to the troops who are actually engaged in battle. What gives? The troops in battle disagree with the Left, that's what.

I do think it's appropriate to debate and discuss how we achieve the biggest, swiftest, and most complete victory. How come the Left doesn't want to discuss this, though? How come, Jess, the questions are always something like yours: "Do you support the war?" ... "Should we get out?," etc. I think such a view is defeatist and irresponsible. Almost all of our troops agree, for what it's worth. Unlike me, a former military member whose thoughts are no more worthy of consideration than any one's on this subject, I do think the views of the men kicking in the doors in Iraq are very relevant as to how politicians are affecting their morale.

Final point and question about military status: What difference does it make that I am former member of the military? The foregoing opinions draw upon my experiences to a degree, and thus have some credibility to this extent. But I don't believe that my service entitles me to some "super opinion" status. This is a mistake that the Left routinely makes now, I think, because they can't substantively defend their position. People such as Kerry, Murtha, and even McCain are afforded "untouchable" status simply because of their service. This is wrong. Opinions should stand on their own. McCain, Murtha, Kerry, et al., have no idea of what needs to be done on the ground in Iraq. Their confident pronouncements of various battle plans (all of which are different, interestingly enough) prove my point. I trust the field commanders. They have all the information, and the expertise.

You asked me what I would do as commander-in-chief. As for the actual fighting of the war, this is a matter to be left to the commanders on the ground. At home, though, I would make the case every day about what is at stake and how we are fighting Militant Islamists. I would highlight their atrocities (which are legion) and implore the Muslim world to take a firm stand against Zarqawi, al Qaeda, et al. The stakes, the reality of the situation in Iraq, and the tangible progress need to be discussed and explained to people much better. This is the one thing in particular I would like to see the Bush Administration do much better.

When the American people are unified, we always win ... and big.

6 September 2008

BTW, though the execution of the Iraq War was in deep trouble pre-surge, …it would be incredibly wrong to concede that going into Iraq itself was wrong.

People need to be reminded of the context of the decision-making process and the near-universal belief that Saddam Hussein had weapons

128

of mass destruction —along with a history of using them —with 9/11 clearly visible at that time in the rearview mirror.

The trouble is ... A lot of people now evaluate the Iraq War as if 9/11 never happened and/or it was ancient history at the time we invaded Iraq. With the information we had at the time, it was the right move to go into Iraq. The real debate was how to prevail and then come home. McCain, to his credit, was the nation's best leader on this issue. I don't believe it is political hyperbole to say that Iraq would have been lost without him pressing the surge.

Meanwhile, Obama now admits the surge worked (though he voted against it), but still ... can't bring himself to say he was wrong. Messiahs don't tend to err, you know.

DC Shutdown: The one constant during the Iraq War was that our troops performed honorably and well, as they always have done. I still believe that it is misguided to vociferously criticize the military's mission while our troops are in harm's way. But I also believe we have a duty to vigorously debate the mission before we go to war, and Congress needs to cease abdicating its duty to declare war. If we cannot explain the national security interest in two to three sixth-grade-level sentences, then we probably are not acting in the national interest. Put another way, it is a moral imperative to only expend one of our nation's most precious resources—the very lives of our troops—if the nation's security compels it.

As for the decision to go war, I now believe that, though the intelligence information apparently warranted the invasion, the inability to locate WMD stockpiles demonstrates in retrospect that the invasion was unnecessary. That is, just because "all 17 intelligence agencies" are purportedly in agreement (as they are on certain current issues) doesn't mean they are above being questioned by the American public or its representatives. Additionally, the effort at nation-building was ill-advised and created a vacuum ultimately leading to the rise of ISIS and an increase of instability and Iranian influence in the region. The war thus showed some of the folly and dangers associated with globalism, as Pres. Trump has long articulated.

While in the last decade our government was focused on promoting interests and controlling borders in the Middle East, the conservative base of the Republican Party began to demand a similar respect for American interests and sovereignty. In the next chapter, I discuss the philosophy undergirding the need to protect our border and preserve the unique character of America.

Chapter Nine

All in All We're Just Another Brick in the Wall

28 November 2005

If you can't draw a line around it, or define it, is it a nation?

Saw an interesting immigration story over the weekend that made page one in our local MSM fishwrap, The *Houston Chronicle.* ...

While presenting the conflicting viewpoints, the gist of the story was that small border towns like Penitas, Texas are being overrun by illegals. Also, the Chronicle reported criticism of the nonsensical policy of local police departments refusing to assist in border enforcement. This "See No Evil" policy has apparently been promoted and condoned by the feds. However, local officials in major metropolitan areas such as Houston are also loath to crack down on illegals for a variety of reasons, both political and economic.

And speaking of political and economic reasons to oppose reform, according to the Pew Hispanic Center and the Dept. of Homeland Security, the civilian workforce is currently comprised of 4.3% illegal aliens. Isn't this about the current unemployment rate?

You know it's gotten bad if discussion of immigration has now reached Washington, even if we are approaching an election year. The Homeland Security Department is reporting that the "catch and release" policy is no more. Also, last year in Texas alone, nearly a half-million illegals were detained, an increase of 22% over the previous year. Even Hillary Clinton is talking about immigration. Note that I said "talking." Yet, if you think she would actually do anything about it, well then you are one of those uninformed voters she will be courting in '08. But you're reading here, so never mind.

While most serious proposals on the issue have come from conservative Republicans, the fact is that neither party has done much of anything on the immigration front. It's been a non-issue in Washington. Why is that?

I think we need look no farther than the awkward coalition of business interests that simply seek the cheapest labor possible (regardless of the source or consequence) and leftists who simply want new minority voters and social service consumers. This big business-big government coalition —aka the Demo-RINOs —is held together by its core principle of disregarding the nation for its own selfish interests. The Demo-RINO coalition also has its own grand immigration plan, a bill sponsored by Ted Kennedy and the RINO-in-Chief himself, John McCain [McCain-Kennedy-Bush].

Plus, with the number of liberal Demo and RINO senators, there are enough votes in the Senate to hold back any serious reform measure. So, while the debate has been raging in the hinterlands, it's been hard to get off the hallowed ground of the World's Most August Deliberative Body.

Furthermore, unlike how the critics wish to market this important debate, race is not the issue. In fact, most Hispanics favor curbing illegal immigration.

At the core, I believe that the debate on immigration is about the following question: Do we wish to preserve and protect this nation or not? Ultimately, true immigration reform will be passed only if we engage and win the debate over the meaning and value of this nation.

To the crowd who simply doesn't care who lives and works here, America is merely a cool spot on a map. It is a place to get a job or do business (get money) or a place to receive benefits (get money). But is this all that America has become —a free-admission version of the Greatest Show on Earth? Where all can be had and all senses are titillated at all hours, free of charge? Is this it?

If so, then we are finished. To win the ongoing national debates over immigration and (on the broader level) national security as a whole, we must know: What is America? And why is the survival of America important? In other words, why is America worth fighting for? If we, as a nation, can't confidently answer these questions, then we won't be able to stop illegal immigration.

I would submit that America is worth preserving because it is a special place, not merely geographically but rather in human history. This nation is not perfect, but it is undeniably special and unique. And if there are no requirements for entry into this nation, as with any organization or institution, then it will naturally lose its special character. Put another way, if America means everything, then it means nothing.

The good news is that the opposite is also true: When we know who we are, we will act accordingly.

Unlike other nations, America's founding charter is really a credo: All men are created equal, with certain God-given rights. Government's role is limited to protecting those individual rights.

This unique experiment in human history is worthy of protection. Still, not all Americans seem to be convinced, or at least to possess the will and courage to fight for what they know to be true.

Years ago, I had a discussion with a friend who had gone to work for Motorola. I was decrying Japanese companies that were blatantly and openly stealing U.S. chip technology. His response was somewhat ambivalent: "It's all the same world. What does it matter?" In other words, why is America so special among nations? Why does this nation's success and survival matter?

Well, maybe one can say we are the same. People are, for sure. But nations are not. Certainly, not every nation would rebuild its vanquished enemy's homeland after winning a world war. And not every nation would conquer Saddam Hussein's Iraq at the cost of more than 2,000 lives and hundreds of billions of dollars, and then help Iraqis set up a democracy.

Other nations might. But America does.

She's worthy of defending.

3 April 2006
The International Gold Standard: U.S. Citizenship

Lots of angst in the air these days. As for me, I am encouraged to see the debate taking place in the country on immigration. It is occurring simultaneously with an ongoing national security debate focusing on Iraq and the larger War on Militant Islam. This is good.

Why? What does a good liberal have to offer in these debates? Not much other than, "Nah, that won't work" ... "Bad idea" ... "Bush lied" ... "We'll get OBL" ... "working wage" ... Oh, come on.

In serious times, the old stand-bys of the minority party are harder to peddle.

Still, on the issue of immigration reform, solving the problem remains difficult because of the deep transnationalism that grips Washington, the intelligentsia/think tank types, the entire Democratic Party, and a number of Republicans, as well.

To me, it boils down to this: Is America a special place, worthy of protection as a distinct nation?

To the trans-nationalist, the honest answer is "no." ...

To me, the crux of the matter in the illegal immigration debate is my belief that America is worthy of protection. As such, citizenship matters. Being an American is more than a geographical quirk warranting endless, hand-wringing guilt. ...

All people are of equal value. But not all nations are equally good.

I would like to posit that the world would be better off if North Korea and Iran were more like the United States, and not the other way around. What sane person would trade their U.S. citizenship for North Korean citizenship?

And closer to home, Mexico's government and economy should look more like the United States' and not the other way around. Can't we acknowledge this? Americans can, but trans-nationalists stammer.

"But the U.S. is not perfect ... blah, blah, blah." Yet again, these utopians in search of perfection in their adversaries on this earth rob the world of its goodness.

Also, while arguing moral equivalency, the transnationalists and multiculturalists continue to foist more schemes upon America to fulfill their own prophecies of the flawed nature of American society, that is, per John Leo, to "deconstruct the traditional historical narrative" of the United States.

Citizenship is the currency of a nation. If the transnationalists print up citizenship papers for all comers, though, then we are bankrupt.

1 May 2006

A Day Without DC

I see we have a "Day Without Immigrants" planned for today. This is interesting. First off, these people are largely not immigrants. Most are not here to assimilate, learn the language, respect our culture, and stay. Most are here simply to work and take what they can, usually back to their home country. They simply want to get theirs in the United States of Meal Tickets.

These are not immigrants. These are "illegals seeking benefits." If the left and the overly sensitive/McCain crowd don't appreciate "illegal alien" (which is absolutely accurate), then how about "illegals seeking benefits?" It seems accurate and appropriate. If they're not seeking benefits, then how about we agree they don't get any? I suspect this won't work.

It is strange indeed to watch the Chamber of Commerce and the Left suddenly find common ground on this issue —their borderless self-interest. For most of us, it's frustrating to see this nation treated like a cafeteria.

So, I say, let these "illegals seeking benefits" walk off the job, school, etc. ... and arrest and deport them. No, we can't ship out all those who are here illegally, I understand. But maybe we can get the militants.

And further in response to the "Day without Illegals Seeking Benefits," I am going to up the ante. Yes, I am going to bring the MOAB: A "Day without DC" tomorrow. That'll teach 'em.

24 May 2007

Immigration ... My Simple Take

Science ... the material is too hard for me. Math ... I am too lazy to do the work. Full-blown philosophy ... too much thinking.

Okay, so let's try "arm-chair" philosophy, with some sweeping generalizations and such.

Seriously, I think I've got something here on the immigration debate.

The proponents and opponents of immigration "reform" are lined up in their various camps based upon how they view America and its ideas and values.

Let me explain.

On the pro-"reform" side, we have big business and big government types. Big business says it needs, but really it wants, cheap labor. Meanwhile, the Hard Left/Big Government coalition sees a huge block of new voters.

The pro-"reform" camp doesn't think much of dimwitted patriots like me. The big business, blue-bloods chuckle their erudite chuckles at my simple-mindedness for thinking that this nation is a place worth preserving, at the expense of the market. To them, the U.S. is merely a market. The Left, meanwhile, sneers at me and my ilk, seeing me not only as thick-headed but also malevolent, for the Hard Left believes that America is the chief obstacle for redistributing the world's resources on the basis of the oligarchs' better judgment, er, need. To the Left, the U.S. is the obstacle.

So, the Left and the Blue Bloods are in bed together, united by their disdain for small-minded Americans who want to see their nation survive.

On the other side ... we have the "anti-reformers," if you will, people like me. These people want existing laws enforced before we create others. We believe that a nation must have a credible border, if it is to survive. We believe that America is a good place, a place where the rights of men are protected as well as any place on the planet.

We believe in playing by the rules. We believe in the power of individuals. We believe that individuals who play by the rules can and still do achieve great things here in America.

We believe in free enterprise; thus, we are skeptical of large bureaucratic institutions, including those that call themselves businesses. To us, free enterprise doesn't mean that business should be able to seek a profit while disregarding the nation's laws.

We don't trust the government on the border. We have heard it all, and the government's credibility reservoir on this subject was drained dry long ago.

And, finally, in the anti-"reform" caucus, we have room for honest liberals who see the importation of a permanent, uneducated underclass into the United States for the exploitation that it is.

We still believe in America.

So let me sum it up: The anti-"reformers" like me are united by their belief in American ideals, while the "reformers" (do words mean anything, any more?) oppose these same ideals.

To me, it's that simple. …

8 June 2007

That Iceberg the Comprehensive Immigration Reform Bill Just Hit …

… may have done the trick. I think I was one of the first to say … it ain't happenin.' It might happen at some point in the future, but this bill looks to be officially dead.

All you naysayers, I know, are ready to be mad about the bill that Hillary is going to sign, with a Democrat Congress in '09. Sure, it may happen. But it might not. Point is, it looks like the disaster that is the "Comprehensive Immigration Reform Bill" du jour has been averted.

As people who know America and her borders are worth protecting, we ought to believe enough in our people to rise up when it matters. Keep the faith.

With this bill and the audacious way that the Senate attempted to foist it on us, without their gigantic monstrosity even being read

("Trust us, we're from the government, we're here to help you, and we really mean it this time when we say that this is the last amnesty, and we'll get right on that fence."), now the tenor of the debate has changed.

For they were caught in the night, trying to steal across what remains of an America that cares about its border.

The message from the majority of Americans, not simply troglodytes like me, is: Enforce the current laws and add true enforcement measures to keep out illegals while punishing businesses who violate the law. Then, we can talk re: what to do next. If the Congress would simply take this approach, many people would be open to a discussion as to what we do with those illegals who are already here. However, the continuing unwillingness to discuss meaningful border enforcement means that people don't believe what their government tells them on this subject, and the mistrust is as deep as ever.

Start with enforcing the border meaningfully, with a fence, a means to track everyone in the U.S., and with punitive measures for those businesses who hire illegals. Then we can actually know how many illegals we really have to deal with. Failure to enforce the border first is a ruse to create a bigger problem, because it's not much of a "problem" anyway in the eyes of the proponents of McCain-Kennedy-Bush. But if we enforce the border and punish those who treat the U.S. like a supermarket, then a lot of the illegals won't come and won't need the perks they are currently being offered via "comprehensive immigration reform." That's the dirty little secret that a lot of McCain-Bush-Kennedy proponents don't want people to know.

But hey ... we've got them outnumbered, as recent events have demonstrated. Don't kid yourself: As I said here a while ago, politicians can be influenced if they think they will lose their jobs. They really can. That's the way the system works here ... still.

19 June 2007
Be Ye Encouraged

... Our side has the better arguments. Check this out from Charles Krauthammer (who apparently didn't get the Fox News memo to pledge fealty to Kennedy-Bush-McCain):

> Why am I so suspicious about the fealty of the reformers to real border control? In part because of the ridiculous debate over the building of a fence. Despite the success of the border barrier in the San Diego area, it appears to be very important that this success not be repeated. The current Senate bill provides for the fencing of no more than one-fifth of the border and the placing of vehicle barriers in no more than one-ninth.
>
> Instead, we are promised all kinds of fancy, high-tech substitutes —sensors, cameras, unmanned aerial vehicles —and lots more armed chaps on the ground to go chasing those who get through.
>
> Why? A barrier is a very simple thing to do. The technology is well tested. The Chinese had success with it, as did Hadrian. In our time, the barrier Israel has built has been so effective in keeping out intruders that suicide attacks are down more than 90 percent.
>
> Fences work. That's why people have them around their houses —not because homeowners are unwelcoming but because they insist that those who wish to come into their domain knock at the front door.

If you want to know where a debate is and is going, look at both the arguments being made and the people making them. …

Note: It is ironic to note the late, great Charles Krauthammer (later a fairly consistent critic of Pres. Trump) to be making one of the best arguments for the wall … nearly a decade prior to the Trump Administration.

3 July 2007

On Immigration … Getting Offensive

… [P]laying "offense" on immigration reform is going to be much more difficult. Some in the Senate (most notably liberal Demos) have sworn that no "enforcement-only" bills will ever pass Congress. Never mind the fact that this is exactly what an overwhelming majority (in the 70-75% range) wants: Enforce the border and U.S. immigration laws first. Then, we can decide how to handle the illegals who are here.

The opponents of real immigration reform have dug in. They know that defense is easier than offense.

So, what now?

We continue to persuade, to inform, and to educate. We continue to reach out to people who might not agree with us on all issues but can work with us on the issue at hand. And when appropriate, we remind our elected representatives that we are watching and, though they may not behave like elephants, we have pachyderm-like memories.

In the end, conservatives who want the border enforced are going to have to find some "strange bedfellows" along the way. Want an example? How about labor unions? I have some profound disagreements with labor unions about many things, but I share their skepticism for the creeping internationalism in U.S. business that ignores responsibility to the nation that makes the cash registers ring, or beep, whatever they do now. I am finding myself agreeing with unions more and more regarding their concerns over the disrespect shown to the American worker by American business. This is just an example of a potential ally in this specific fight.

To play offense successfully, we need to find common ground and build coalitions. Hey, I think there's something on the banner of this blog that might speak to this. …

So, can we be both winsome and shrewd? I think we can. Ronald Reagan was. Remember the Reagan Democrats? They helped to elect Reagan when the Republicans were a minority party.

Conservatives shouldn't be surprised that they are in the minority, but neither should they be discouraged.

It's not mutually exclusive to be good and smart. Thus, we should be "wise as serpents and innocent as doves."

DC Shutdown: So, I was for a wall before it was cool. To be fair, even some Demos were. But that was in another time. Now, those seeking border enforcement are part of a coalition made up of the conservative Republican base, disaffected Demos, union members, and other newcomers to the electoral process who put country above the interests of mere merchants and political operators. In the next chapter, I leave the world of politics and have a little fun with some of the most popular posts at Daisy Cutter—those dealing with monumental sporting and weather events. In doing so, we get a glimpse of the heart of the culture of our great land.

Chapter Ten

Perfect Storm

Sports and Texas Weather

23 June 2006

Confessions of an American Heathen —Soccer is not a Sport

… Lots of interesting things happening in the world, i.e., a terror ring busted in Miami, another senior jihadi nabbed in Iraq (good thing there are no jihadis there), the House okays the line-item veto, the Demos in '06 have found their theme: Run on Cut-n-Run, … etc.

But let's talk about something really important —soccer. Why talk about a game? Well, dear reader, this is not a game. It's a religion. And I take great personal risk by criticizing it.

Let's be honest. After all, if you cannot tell when something is ever going to end (does the game clock mean nothing? Who mercifully calls the game "over?"), if there is no scoring, and if only the faithful understand the majesty and mystery of the enterprise while the majority looks on in disbelief and complete befuddlement, then what you have is much more akin to a bad sermon than a sport.

Let me just say that I always pull for our American teams, and I certainly wasn't hoping for the U.S. to get eliminated from the World Cup by Ghana … GHANA!!! How does America lose in anything to Ghana?!! Ah, more proof that soccer is not a real sport. If it's a real sport, America cares enough about it to win. And we never lose to Ghana.

Take curling for example. Now that is a sport —clearly-defined objective, easily understood, scoring occurs, and Americans are good at it. The Canadians are tough, but there is nothing like watching a pair of husky Minnesota girls work those brooms at 90 mph. At any rate, as you can tell, I am a big curling afficionado, and I digress. My apologies ...

The silver lining in the American elimination from the World Cup is that perhaps we will get less soccer evangelism here now. We can only hope.

I know I have breathed heresy on this blog now —finally —by daring to criticize soccer. I know that my simpleton American mind doesn't get the beauty of a bunch of foreigners running/jogging (it's great exercise, you know, and you couldn't do it, anyway ... try getting banged on the dome with a soccer ball) all over a large green field and occasionally kicking/running into a ball. WILL SOMEONE GRAB THAT BALL, AND RUN OVER THE GOALIE AND SCORE?!! AT LEAST DRAW A FOUL!!! DO SOMETHING!!!!!). Why does the goalie get to wear whatever he wants, anyway? And then ... all of this aimless running around is on rare occasions interrupted (once a game, if you're lucky) by someone knocking the ball into the net. (This, too, apparently happens on accident with some frequency.)

And then some foreigner rips his shirt off and runs around the field screaming. I don't get it. I know, it's a beautiful mystery and I am an obtuse lout.

I don't understand the beauty of the insurmountable 1-0 lead.

I don't understand the passion that necessitates the throwing of blood and urine bombs at soccer "matches." There's another strike against soccer. It's a "match," not a game.

I don't understand a sport where you knock someone over and they give you a "card." I mean, in a real sport, you take out one of our players and you get hit in the coconut with the ball, taken to the deck, or taken out of the game.

I don't understand soccer hooligans. In soccer, the baddest guys don't even play. Is it the "passion?" No, just more insanity associated with soccer. But I am still interested in who will take the "Hoolicup." At least the hooligans have the sense to interrupt a soccer MATCH with some excitement.

I don't understand why soccer people can't just let this baseball/football/basketball fan be. I love a football field. It's marked in yards. And a baseball diamond ... it's marked in feet.

I'm wondering ... Are these soccer people the same ones that were peddling the metric system in America, telling us that we would be left in the Dark Ages if we didn't imitate Europe and the rest of the "civilized" world?

I don't understand why all those soccer people feel the need to schedule their religious services (er, matches) on Sunday mornings. Never mind.

I don't understand how you can't express dissent about soccer without getting some version of soccer evangelism shoved at you. I mean, if you don't like baseball or football, I know something is wrong with you. I don't need to tell you about it. Just like if you are soccer fanatic, you have told me enough. Say no more. Stop preaching and show me some of that European-like relativism.

I think these soccer people like soccer because America is not good at soccer.

But that's okay. I just think the fact that we're not good at it and the nation shrugs when we get eliminated from the World Cup shows ...

Soccer doesn't matter.

But I am just an American heathen.

20 October 2005

So, What is the Answer to Pujols' Crushing HR in Game 5?

Roy Oswalt. He's a 5' 11," 175 lb. ball of fire from Weir, Mississippi. Meet the NLCS MVP and the Cardinals' worst nightmare.

Long before 28-year-old Roy Oswalt was born, many Houston fans were spending their Octobers watching the heavyweights of baseball in the World Series. No more. Chicago, here we come.

As my sons started looking ahead to the World Series in the ninth inning last night, I chastised them again for their youthful exuberance. Monday night's crushing loss was just the latest in a long line of disappointing Astros' playoff foibles. Then, to my horror, Fox put up

"Astros @ Chicago" for World Series Game 1, before the last out was recorded. I chastised Fox accordingly, and then Mark Grudzilanek got a solid single to left. More nerves. Then, the majestic routine fly ball to right field was snared by Jason Lane …

My immediate comment in the aftermath: "I still can't believe the President nominated Harriet Miers." No really, here is what I said: "If you live long enough, you'll see everything."

I then started going over my Astros memories … I remember my first game at the Astrodome, which was way ahead of its time in the 1960s. I remember a short power hitter, Jimmy Wynn, the "Toy Cannon." I remember Enos Cabell, Craig Reynolds, and the first left-side of the infield that I could remember cheering for: Roger Metzger and Doug "the Rooster" Rader. Tommy Helms and Lee May rounded out that infield. But they never made the playoffs. That was for other teams.

My first "Astro Buddy" [Fan Club for Kids] was a skinny kid pitcher named Larry Dierker, still the team's all-time leader in wins. I still remember when he threw his no-hitter. He was a workhorse, and I cheered when he was hired as manager. But I like Phil Garner just fine, too. The guy who hired them both, Drayton McLane, is just one of those optimistic guys who wears on you initially, but then you see that he really means it. He has said "champion" so many times around here that Houstonians just roll their eyes. They're not rolling eyes any more.

I remember summer nights with the radio and the unflappable Gene Elston. And there was the late and great, Loel "he breezed him one more time" Passe. Gene was so cool, but I remember one meaningless game in the dog days where the Astros scored 6 runs with two outs in the bottom of the ninth to beat the Expos, 6-5. Gene was so excited; he was just screaming. I was, too.

In 1980, they scored 7 runs with two outs in the ninth in Montreal to beat the Expos again. What a hoot. Almost as big a hoot as listening to Milo "I am the play-by-play guy, but I bet you can't guess the score" Hamilton. My boys and I have gotten many kicks through the years as Milo continues to pile up the follies and wear out his supply of cliches. He is especially funny when griping out the Astros after a loss. Or when he forgets how many outs there are. Or when he forgets that we can't see what's happening, so we need someone who can to tell us.

There I was as a kid on opening day, watching in a packed Astrodome as a young pitcher named Mark Lemongello (yes, Lemongello) baffled the Dodgers and the Astros won, 4-3, in 10 innings. Later, I would take my boys to the same Astrodome to teach them the game and teach them to cheer for our team —the Astros. One Father's Day, we took my dad to the Dome and he couldn't believe the boys' knowledge and interest in the game. ...

All those years ... all those players. The sweet swing of Terry Puhl, the multi-talented Cesar Cedeno, the clutch Bob "the Bull" Watson, Don Wilson, Cliff Johnson, Joe Morgan, Jose Cruz, Denny Walling, Jesus Alou, Dickie Thon, Moises Alou, Charlie "all the NY fans cuss, are drunk, and have black teeth, and that's just the women" Kerfeld, Dave Smith, Joe Sambito, Joe Niekro, Bob Knepper, Billy Doran, Ken Caminiti, Mike Hampton, Alan Ashby, Darryl Kile ... There was some guy from Alvin who pitched here for a while, yeah, Nolan Ryan.

I remember seeing a young kid who played catcher. Man, he could run for a catcher. I thought ... "this kid can play." His name: Biggio. And I recall a trade of one of my favorite relief pitchers, Larry Anderson, for a pretty good young hitter, Jeff Bagwell.

Man, you've gotta be happy for Biggio and Bagwell.

One night I saw Bagwell hit a wayward slider from Byun Yung Kim seemingly all the way to Galveston to win a ballgame. I also saw Baggy in the strike-shortened 1994 season, and he was every bit as good as any hitter around today ... including Pujols. He won the league MVP then and hit something like .368 with 37 homers in a shortened season. Incredible.

I was there at the Dome on a Friday night in 1986; the Astros blew a 3-run lead in the ninth inning when Darryl Strawberry homered. But my all-time favorite Astro, Craig Reynolds, hit a game winning homer in the bottom of the ninth. From there, the Astros went on their incredible run to the NLCS against the Mets. They got there with the incredible division-clinching no-hitter by Mike Scott.

I remember the depressing loss in the 1980 LCS. Tal Smith, the … GM then, is still the team's president. I felt the exhilaration of Billy Hatcher's game-tying bomb in the 14th inning of the 1986 LCS, and the sting of Kevin Bass's strikeout in the 16th to end it.

The LCS losses in 1980 and 1986 were both to eventual World Series Champions.

I remember when they drafted some hefty outfielder from Rice. But that kid Berkman could hit.

I was there when Randy Johnson threw his first game as an Astro in 1998 … a complete game shutout over the Phillies. That 1998 team may have been the best Astro team ever, with a playoff rotation of Johnson, Hampton, and Lima … and a flame-throwing closer named Wagner. There have always been great pitchers in an Astro uniform.

I have seen playoff collapses year after year … I was there in 1999, the last season in the Astrodome, when Walt Weiss made "the play" on a bases-loaded shot by Tony Eusebio; 52,000 thousand people gasped, and the Astros collapsed. The Braves won the game and the series on the next day at the Dome. I was in the stands then for the last game ever played at the Dome. I've been in the stands twice when the Braves eliminated the Astros in the playoffs.

I was there on Opening Day at Enron Field in 2000. Man, what a bad season that was. The pitchers were shell-shocked and psyched out by the new ballpark, as opposing hitters salivated. The last few years, my boys and I have had some great days and nights at the stadium that has become Minute Maid Park. They win every time we go. We're going to Game 5 of the WS. The Rocket will be on the mound.

I remember when the Astros signed Andy Pettitte in '03, and then later Andy coaxed his buddy Roger to join him. Then, we started dreaming again around here. It was just too much to resist. And the Rocket lifted the team, almost immediately.

Indeed, last year, even with Pettitte hurt, the Astros traded for Carlos Beltran and went all the way to Game 7 of the NLCS. I remember watching as Jeff Kent hit his walk-off homer in Game 5. We dared to believe. But it was all for naught, as the Cards won it in 7.

Earlier this season, my sons' baseball team went to watch the Astros on May 31. They played pretty well and beat the Reds, 4-3, behind Galveston's Brandon Bakke on that warm night. That win made them 19-32. The very next day, however, the *Houston Chronicle* pronounced them dead, saying that the focus should be on next year. The team was laden with too many young players, too many old players, indeed too many question marks. Bagwell was hurt.

They were dead alright. Like Lazarus.

Later this season, we also saw them beat the Rockies. And ... oh, yeah, we were there on the last day of the season when they clinched. Some guy named Oswalt was on the mound. Bedlam.

But when the incomparable Albert Pujols hit his devastating moon shot on Monday night, all the pain of the past came back in an instant. The Astros were given up for dead ... again.

But this team had come too far to die. It had the best "big 3" starting rotation in baseball ... Oswalt, Pettitte, and the Rocket. And they had the best closer in baseball, Brad Lidge —a great pitcher and a better young man. Morgan Ensberg had become an All-Star and Lance Berkman recovered from knee surgery to continue to pick up clutch hits down the stretch. Mike Lamb stepped up big. Jason Lane had a huge, breakthrough year. Biggio's bat looked quicker than ever. And the role players ... Everett, Ausmus, Wheeler, Burke, Astacio, Qualls, Gallo, Bruntlett, Rodriguez, Springer, Vizcaino, Palmeiro, Bakke, Taveras, and (this year) Bagwell ... filled their roles.

But the bottom line was: The team's stellar pitching staff just wouldn't let this team lose. As a result, they had the best record in baseball from mid-May through the end of the season. And they needed every single win just to make the playoffs, as they edged the Phillies by a solitary game for the Wild Card.

The other night, after the Astros were given up "for dead" again, I commented to my boys that if the Astros got by the Cards, the adversity in Game 5 could actually make it more likely that they would win the World Series.

It seems possible now. Because if you live long enough ...

Note: While Game 5 of the 2017 World Series (eventually won by the Astros) was a game for the ages, there was no Game 5 of the 2005 World Series. The Astros were swept by the White Sox.

5 February 2007

But more important than that …

Very much enjoyed the Colts' victory last night, as it represented vindication for Tony Dungy and Peyton Manning. I am big fans of both, especially Dungy. I like Lovie Smith, too, but I was really pulling for Tony Dungy.

For those that don't know, Coach Dungy lost his 18-year-old son to suicide last season. His team rallied around him, but they were eliminated from the playoffs by the Steelers in '05. Repeatedly, he's had to endure the standard refrain that he and his team are "soft" and incapable of competing with the big, bad Patriots and the tough-minded, ever-dour Bill Belichek.

But Tony Dungy has always been a picture of class. He has never wavered. He never lashed back at critics. He is always gracious. Can a leader of men be thus?

Well, it appears so. This year he vanquished Belichek and the "unbeatable" Tom Brady.

Then, much was made of the Super Bowl matchup between Dungy and Smith, for it was they were the first-ever black head coaches to lead their teams to the Super Bowl. Now, Dungy has made history by becoming the first black head coach to win a title.

And it couldn't have happened to a better guy. He was gracious in fielding questions all week about the historic matchup with his friend Smith. Dungy gave Smith his first job in the NFL, after all. Both of the coaches told the press how it was indeed a big deal to be the first two black head coaches to make it to the game's biggest stage. Both are a lot alike, and they have this strange, almost antiquated notion today that you don't have to act like an idiot to be a leader. Heck, you don't even need to curse.

Along the way, the MSM ignored the biggest story of all. You see, these two superior coaches at the top of their craft are not only black, not only great friends ... they are also committed Christians.

How can this be, pray tell? The MSM saw a more important angle in the matchup, and as noted above, it's not that it wasn't important.

It's just that the MSM missed the most important thing, like they usually do. Their template doesn't allow them to see what others do.

I saw some of Coach Dungy's interviews this week, and he credited those black coaches who came before who didn't get the opportunity he did. He graciously offered that better coaches never got the chance he did. And he may be right.

But better men didn't get the chance.

So, it's only fitting that the first black head coach to win an NFL title is Tony Dungy, the Christian. Here's a man who (a year removed from losing his son) still expresses his gratitude to God. Amazing.

At the end of the game, Jim Nance asked Coach Dungy for his thoughts on being the first black head coach to win it. All week long, the coach had tried to tell those who would listen that there was something more to this story. After Nance asked the question with the world watching, Dungy acknowledged his pride. And then he said something like this: "But more important than that, this game shows that you can succeed doing as Christian coaches doing it the right way. Lovie Smith and I are committed Christian coaches who do it the right way."

This was the most important message from the coach. I cheered from my living room.

And Black History Month was honored in a way that many could have only dreamed.

It can be done the right way. And we were reminded of that by a giant of a man who happens to be black. I may not be black, and I may not be related by blood, but I am as proud as can be of my brother in the faith —Tony Dungy.

5 January 2006

From the Once-Again Football Capitol of the World ... a Night of Merriment

A few thoughts after taking and making congratulatory calls from friends near and far, and even from some in the Rose Bowl last night:

First, it was probably the best football game I have ever seen. Hard to think of a better one, especially with more at stake. Vince was just simply masterful, truly a man playing with the boys of Troy.

For his part, Matt Leinart recovered from a difficult first half against a harassing Texas defense to absolutely light up the Longhorns' tremendous defenders in the second half. Reggie Bush was mostly held in check this night, except for one nearly gravity-defying 30-yard touchdown run. His first-half lateral attempt was an ill-advised and uncharacteristic mental error.

For Texas, Super Man was Super Man. But others made huge plays, too. For instance, there was Michael Griffin's incredible end zone interception, the only pick ever thrown by Leinart in a bowl game. Tight end David Thomas was both steady and spectacular, with 10 catches. Ramonce Taylor broke loose for a key touchdown run, and freshman Jamaal Charles finally stopped dropping footballs for a while to flash some brilliance. Michael Huff was everywhere.

USC's Lendale White made all the big runs. Except one. For the first time in the second half, Texas defense rose up to stop the huge bruiser on fourth and two with a little more than two minutes left. He was chatting it up on the sideline a bit too early, it seems.

Then, Vince took the Horns home by scoring on fourth down with 19 seconds left. Bedlam ensued in the Rose Bowl.

And all across Texas living rooms like mine.

The post-game class of Pete Carroll was striking. But Pete is always that way. He is a super coach, a great credit to USC and to college football. Incidentally, Texas has a coach like that, too. And I guess we can now officially put to rest the claims that Coach Brown can't win the big game. ...

So, no, Mack didn't win the big game. His team just won the biggest ever.

USC QB Matt Leinart was pouty and ungracious in some of his post-game comments (i.e., "the best team did not win tonight"). Vince Young, a similarly fierce competitor, was similarly ungracious after Bush's Heisman win, though. UT fans love Vince, so we can forgive Matt Leinart.

It just doesn't get much better than coming from 12 points behind with 6 minutes left to beat the supposedly unbeatable Trojans, the team for the ages and winners of 34 straight. And to do it in Southern California, in SC's hometown and in the shadow of Disneyland is, well, magical.

I remember the last Texas national championship. It was 1970, when the Longhorns were AP Champions, like USC was two years ago. In those days, the votes were counted before the bowl games, so the devastating Notre Dame defeat in the Cotton Bowl (which stopped a 30-game Texas win streak) did not cost the Longhorns the AP title that year.

The last undisputed Texas football championship, though, was in 1969. I remember that one, too, because the '69 championship really felt like Texas was on top of the college football world. That's because the Longhorns were.

I told my 15-year-old before he went to bed early this morning to enjoy this championship. My son may be 50 when it happens again, and I may be dead.

But for now, Texas football is again king.

Note: While the Bowl Championship Series (BCS) was a subjective system for putting together the top two teams for the championship game worked well in the 2006 Rose Bowl, it was not kind to the Texas Longhorns in 2008 when they defeated the Oklahoma Sooners but were nonetheless denied the opportunity to play Florida for the national championship. That grave injustice prompted the following column.

8 December 2008

BCS DECLARES GERMANY WINNER OF WW2

—U.S. Ranked 4th

The BCS tries to look at the overall picture, and who would be a more "feared opponent" if the war were to continue even though it had already been fought to a conclusion. As Commissioner Pi explained, "Considering the Germans' entire body of work — including an incredibly tough Strength of Schedule and brutal routs — our computers deemed them worthy of the #1 ranking."

When questioned about the #4 ranking of the United States, Mr. Pi stated, "The US only had two major victories — Japan and Germany. The computer models, unlike humans, aren't influenced or even killed by head-to-head contests. Rationality lives on, and our computers, along with the many German military officers who vote in our 'human-element' polls consider each contest to be only a single, equally-weighted event."

German Chancellor Adolph Hitler, through a spokesman in Iran, said "Yes, we lost to the U.S., infidels, rather invaders; but we defeated #2 ranked France in only six weeks." Hitler had been criticized for seeking dramatic victories to earn "style points" to enhance Germany's rankings. However, Hitler protested: "Our contest with Poland was in doubt until the final day and the conditions in Norway were incredibly challenging and demanded the application of additional forces. In France, we marched in straight lines under the trees along streets so pretty."

The French ranking has also come under intense scrutiny. Commissioner Pi, though, commented that "France had a single loss against Germany, and following a pre-season #1 ranking, they only fell to #2. Plus, although the battle was over relatively quickly in France, the French managed to keep casualties extremely light."

Japan finished ahead of the U.S. in WWII with a #3 ranking, based largely upon its victories including Manchuria, Borneo and the Philippines. Additionally, as of WWII, BCS computers did not account for the effects of a nuclear attack, Pi said.

Note: In addition to several consequential events in the world of sports covered in Daisy Cutter, we on the Gulf Coast also endured a brush from Hurricane Rita and a direct hit by Hurricane Ike. Both events were instructive of the character of the great people of Texas and America.

9/17/08

Which beach would the Candidate of Change identify more with ... Malibu or Galveston?

Greetings, all. We continue to emerge from our hovels around here as life begins to slowly return to normal. Make no mistake, it was bad here on the Texas Gulf Coast. It still is.

The power at our house was restored a short while ago, but about 1.25 million as of this writing remain without power.

There is no delicate way to say this: The national media's coverage of this disaster has been breathtakingly ignorant. It's understandable for many outside the Gulf Coast to think the story line here is that the "storm surge was less than expected." The truth is that, while the surge could have been higher, it was wide and deep. The hurricane made a direct hit on the Houston-Galveston area. Hurricane-force winds in this huge storm blanketed the Houston-Area for hours as about 15 inches of rain fell.

The area looks like a war zone in many spots. Trees and power lines are down everywhere. In much of the Houston area, houses that did not lose trees are the exception. ...

You won't hear a lot nationally from the residents of the Texas Gulf Coast, the same people who shouldered much of the burden of sheltering Katrina refugees. Most will just go on about their business of trying to pick up the pieces of their lives.

Life goes on. Here, we get hit about every 20 years or so with a major hurricane. Since the last one was 25 years ago, I blame global cooling for the 5-year respite.

Lots of politicians have been on the radio the past few days. There's been a little finger-pointing, and certainly some pandering from time to time, as you might imagine. Mostly, the comments and the efforts have been constructive, though. The best line I heard came from Pres. Bush ... who said, "By helping your neighbor, you are helping your nation."

Lots of my neighbors are helping their nation around here. That's how many of them live. On Saturday, one neighbor who I didn't even know showed up with a chainsaw to remove a fallen tree from my driveway. Another showed me how to pump my septic. Others gathered and distributed intel about where to get gas. There were thousands of acts of kindness and generosity that you will never hear about.

There were some isolated pockets of exceptions, but the rule was amazingly-civilized and neighborly conduct around here. Nearly all the stop lights have been out (I mean no lights at all), but people respect each other and the law and treat them like 4-way stops. It's a small thing, but it gives you insight into the deep decency of the people of the Texas Gulf Coast.

Meanwhile, on Galveston Island, the situation is dire. Incidentally, Galveston is a heavily-Democrat area of the state. It seems, though, that the national Democrats don't seems to have much time to spend on Galveston Beach. Surely, this doesn't have anything to do with Texas' shiny red status, does it?

Maybe the many black residents who lost everything on Galveston Island can ask the Candidate of Change at the next opportunity.

But alas, it appears they won't get the opportunity. Obama found a beach in Malibu more to his liking than Galveston. The Barack and Babs gathering of last night speaks volumes, and on many levels.

Trembling markets and the self-anointed change agent of our time simultaneously and ominously announce the weakness of much of our sick, self-absorbed politics and culture.

And the cure won't be found in the government.

The cure is among us ... out in the neighborhoods and in our homes.

The World Through the Eyes of a Houstonian (... or a Weatherman)

Life intervenes again ... so I blog not. Or at least blog not much. Spent Wednesday at a refinery in Beaumont. Funny, but the guys there were pretty sure that Rita was going to hit south of the Houston area, and they would thus be spared. Nonetheless, they were pretty interested in getting hurricane preparations done. It looks like it may have been a good thing.

Hurricane preparations have been going fast and furious here on the Gulf Coast. Frankly, people are a bit panicked, but with the media reports, who can blame them? The hysteria has spilled over such that WalMart doesn't have "D" batteries. Now, that is panic.

But seriously, I have stood back and watched in amazement as hundreds of thousands of cars hit the road ... and then just stopped. No shootings. No mayhem. No crying for Washington to help. Some complaining and grumbling for sure. Understandably so. But people have just been remarkable.

Local officials have been good. Houston Mayor Bill White and Harris County Judge Robert Eckels have been informative and have generally implemented this crazy evacuation plan about as well as you can. Some are griping about the inevitable glitches when evacuating more than a million people, but I think most of us understand that this is one of those "defecation occurs" deals. In other words, when hundreds of thousands of people decide to gas up and hit the trail simultaneously ... Houston, we have a problem.

I left at 6:30 A.M. today in search of batteries and a couple of more lights ... for the inevitable power outage. Also, I was hoping to fill up my truck. Struck out on the gas hunt. But I did manage to get in line at Academy Surplus and snag a couple of lights. While waiting in the Academy parking lot for the store to open, I noticed that I had happened upon a makeshift rest area. People played with dogs. Women slept in cars with mouths wide open. One guy's generator on his trailer hummed loudly while he caught some shut eye. It was like a circus, but people were good-natured and it was a pretty orderly circus.

I found no batteries at Academy. Not even at WalMart. They must not make 'em any more. Everywhere I went, people were in pretty good spirits under the circumstances, although there was some griping when we had to get in line and go into Academy no more than six at a time. Three other guys and I were trying to make a "brotherhood" pact so we could go in as a family ... to no avail.

A few more stops. Still no batteries. No ice. Not much of anything. I mean, even WalMart ran out of bottled water. Okay ... looks like we're at the bottom of the barrel here. No gas. How many stations did I look at? I forgot.

A young man in the WalMart parking lot (basically a campground now) asks me how to get to College Station. We need to talk. Doesn't he know there are Aggies there? He can do better than that. ... I give him my super-secret "around Conroe" directions, all the while keeping him off the dreaded interstate. I have made a new friend. And then he asks: Aren't you going to leave? "No way. We are good up here. Besides, Pres. Bush is going to steer the storm toward Louisiana." Okay, so I didn't say the last part.

It was a day when strangers came together and talked about this memorable event. People asked for help, and it was usually given. A couple drove up beside me and asked for my secret directions to Highway 75. How did they know? I offered my map, but they had one. Maybe they were looking for College Station. Who knows?

The roads here are complete madness. You may have seen the pictures on TV, but it is hard to overstate the chaos and frustration that are the freeways in this area. Usually, they are simply unbearable. The last couple of days they are just insane. Miraculously, there have been no major gun battles. Or even any. Cars run out of gas after idling for hours on the freeways waiting to evacuate. Cars overheat. Some turn off their engines, put the vehicles in neutral and push to save gas. People get out of their cars and take a stroll on the freeway.

I finally arrived back home ... at 3 P.M. ... with a few paltry supplies. It only took me three hours to go about 15 miles to my house.

The AC was used sparingly while waiting in traffic, too. But at least it's only 100 degrees today.

Why do we live here again? Oh, yeah. The invention of the air conditioner. Let's face it, hurricanes are only part of the great climate here.

Yet, these things happen on the Gulf Coast. In 1961, Carla hit. In 1983 —22 years later —Alicia's eye crossed at San Luis Pass in Galveston, and downtown Houston was devastated. Now, another 22 years later, the third most-powerful storm ever churns out in the Gulf.

In spite of all of this, though, we live here because some of the best, heartiest, salt-of-the-earth types you will ever meet call the Texas Gulf Coast their home. I am staying. …

DC Shutdown: Twelve years after Rita when Hurricane Harvey hit, this same grit and character was on display in the Gulf Coast for all the world to see. Then, in 2008 another hurricane was churning off the coast of the nation (other than Ike, that is). That was Hurricane Obama. Sensing the coming storm, I came out of blogger semi-retirement to do what I could to make the case for John McCain. In doing so, I (and many of us conservatives) saw once and for all how our side must draw bold contrasts with the Left … and fight … to have a chance to win.

Chapter Eleven

Moderation in the Pursuit of Victory is no Virtue

The Awkward Dance that was the McCain Campaign Begets the Obama Debacle

13 June 2008

So what now?

I went back and read my launch post for "Blogs for McCain's Opponent." If I do say so myself, I think it was just grand.

I must say that the slicing and dicing of Sen. McCain in my post of three years ago was pretty complete. Yes, I upset the McCainites so bad that the very last commenter called me a Dutch Bagholder. Made my day back then. But what about today?

I'd encourage you to read my "Blogs for McCain's Opponent's" launch post carefully and read it to the end. I never intended then, and I don't intend now, to help a liberal Democrat (or worse) get elected to anything, much less to be the Commander-in-Chief in a time of war.

So, now we find ourselves in a fine predicament, do we not? As conservatives, we certainly can't be fired up about Johnny McCain. We remember ... McCain-Feingold [campaign-finance "reform" bill limiting private speech and further empowering the media] ... the Gang of 14 [that "bipartisan" group of senators who, in 2005, negotiated a deal to preserve the Democrats' ability to filibuster judicial nominations] ... McCain-Kennedy. That last hyphenated McCain mess is the immigration bill/debacle that conservatives derailed in '06. He's been the media's, not conservatives,' darling these past eight years for a reason. ...

All of McCain's foibles (immigration, big media-friendly

legislation, green pandering, etc.) point out that he is the friend of big business, and by extension, big government. That's McCain's common thread and his Achilles' heel with conservatives. Yes, conservatives are aware how the interests of multinational mega-corporations diverge more and more from the national interest. And big gov't, the friend of big biz, well ... that used to mean what it meant to be one of us —that you didn't like empowering the feds to do everything.

But even so, McCain has an opponent. ...

[W]hat do you think? McCain or Obama? That's the choice, you know. One of these two will become president next year. So, don't tell me how many Libertarians can balance on a rolled-up Constitution, or the merits of a Nader candidacy (this is Ralph's year, after all).

Which one should it be —McCain or Obama —and why? These are the questions we face.

26 September 2008

DC on the Bailout ["Emergency Economic Stabilization Act of 2008"] ...

... My position: Opposed. Strongly so. We should pursue an approach along the lines of that advocated by House Republicans (that is, where the government becomes lender, rather than owner, and the taxpayer can be paid back with interest from loans as they perform). This seems to be a sound approach. The Paulson plan is very troubling, and on many levels —i.e., the rush to passage, the government confiscation of a huge sector of the American economy, and the demand that we minions accept the $700 billion approximation of the problem without question or amendment.

1 October 2008

Bailing out Palin

As for the bailout ... I would still vote no, absent a serious move to make the bill more free-market oriented, i.e., loans to troubled financial institutions instead of government ownership of assets or an insurance plan. ...

McCain, meanwhile, is for "bi-partisanship." Please. That begs the question about what we are committed to work on together. I haven't yet been persuaded that the Paulson Plan and its variations are going to prevent the sky from caving in, or even that it is a worthy endeavor in the first place. Aren't we about a week after D-Day, anyway? In my world, people who are asking for $700B and a large stake in the American mortgage industry have the burden of proof, and it's a high one. ...

Let the Demos take credit for this plan, thus, we'll have a coalition of Demos and Bush. The Candidate of Change sides with Bush and McCain sides with us. Now, there's a story. There's the election. Can you imagine the next two presidential debates as McCain hammers Obama for voting for the Bush bailout ... and then Obama tries to break out that 90%-with-Bush nonsense (McCain only sided with Bush when it wasn't a big deal)? McCain says, "There you go again. I oppose Pres. Bush on principle and on weighty matters, and you side with him for political purposes. The American people rightfully and deeply distrust this bailout, and we will reap the consequences for many years. You have shown you are not ready to be president."

But alas, it appears McCain has sided with Blessed Bi-Partisanship. Put your hand over your heart when you read that, understand? You ideological miscreants who put country ahead of getting along, you.

Speaking of the election and letting things happen ... Let Sarah be herself tomorrow night, and she'll likely wipe the floor with Biden. You know and I know that Sarah doesn't wake up in the A.M. filling her lungs with the fresh air of Blessed Bipartisanship and extolling the virtues of Democrats. She would field-dress 'em, if she could.

9 October 2008

DC's Campaign with 25 Days to Go: 25 Reasons to Vote for McCain and Against Obama

Greetings, all. These are important times. I agree with Rush that it looks like conservatives are "going to have to drag McCain" over the finish line. However, today it looks like he has picked it up a bit, in that McC actually named Barney Frank and Chris Dodd for their complicity in the mortgage-financial meltdown.

Four years ago, I broke down John Kerry's anti-American book, *The New Soldier*, in the month leading up the election. I did so because I thought then (and now) that the sentiments expressed by Kerry in the book laid the groundwork for why he could not be allowed to become Commander-in-Chief. In my view, his worldview disqualified him from being president. I made the judgment that Kerry's failure to reverse course on his prior anti-Americanism during the Vietnam War meant that he should not be allowed to lead America. For me, it's pretty straightforward. If you give us good reason to doubt your love for the nation, then it's nonsensical that you should be allowed to lead the nation.

What we saw in Kerry, we see all over again (and then some) in Obama. Actually, the people that Obama is comfortable associating with make Kerry look mild by comparison. Obama is masking a radical agenda with soothing and well-delivered rhetoric.

I am concerned for my country. …

So … I will "come out of retirement" for the next 25 days to do the following: I will provide a short post each day to remind you of one reason to vote for McCain and/or against Obama (if that makes some of you feel better). …

It is on. …

13 October 2008

Day 4/Reason #22: Hanoi Hilton vs. the Harvard Hawaiian

My personal view is that you can tell a lot about people by how they treat those who really can't do much for them in return. A good example of this is found in how people treat waiters, flight attendants, and the like. A corollary here is that our private conduct is much more indicative of the type of person we are than our public conduct.

I read a story the other day about how Obama and his staff treat the press traveling with them like dirt. Mind you, these very same members of the press are true-blue lefties and in the tank for The One.

He-Whose-Defecation-Is-Not-Odiferous, however, no doubt knows that these lefties in the press will surely stay on the team regardless of how he behaves. He doesn't need to be nice to them, so he won't.

McCain, on the other hand, drives many of us on the right mad by trying to show decency to all. He even told angry supporters on Friday that Obama is a decent guy. McC has that famous temper, but it is generally reserved for politicians. They can take it. (It would be nice to see him lay into Demos more, but hey). By all accounts, though, McCain shows decency to most everyone he encounters, whether they be big or "little people."

Ah, but to Obama, we're all little. My conclusion is that the vast gaps in life experience of the two —Hanoi Hilton vs. Hawaii-Harvard-"Community Organizer" … explains this difference.

McCain's life experience has taught him his own personal limits and fallibility. Meanwhile, Obama has been cheered every step of the way as some gift from on-high to all of us lucky beneficiaries. To me, the greatest experience argument against Obama is that life has not tested him in any real way. Rather, life appears to have propped him up, and perhaps given him an inflated view of himself as a result.

As a result of Obama's life experience (or the lack of any real test of leadership), we are left to wonder if Obama has ever been to a place where he only had to rely upon his character and faith for survival. We know McCain has been there.

We should be greatly afraid of a politician who thinks he is better than all of us peons. Arrogance in the small things will show up in the larger things. In stealing our liberty, Obama will know best. …

15 October 2008

Day 6/Reason #20: Imperfect Candidate or Intolerable Government

Conservatives know, or should know, the limits of this world. We should be among the first to eschew perfect churches, organizations, and political campaigns, for in joining them, we ruin them.

McCain is certainly an imperfect candidate, and I have typed a lot of words in this space detailing my views in this regard. But really, at this point, what is the point of such arguments? The very real specter of an Obama presidency looms. The theoretical among us like to argue about what ought to be, but the rest of us have to live with what is and what will be. …

Obama's whole life story shows us that he would lead the nation farther to the left than any president in our history. His government would be a great encroachment on American liberty and livelihood, that is, if his national security policy doesn't get us all killed first. This intolerable government (what will be, not what may be imagined dancing on the heads of pins), this unmitigated disaster, is the alternative to the imperfect candidacy of John McCain.

So … for those conservatives who want to bemoan what might have been or what ought to be in this election season, the rest of us are left here to deal with the here and now.

We must defeat Obama. And a conservative not voting for McCain in this election is, in effect, giving a vote to Obama. Rev. Wright and Co. would like to congratulate and thank you.

Those who whine and look for perfect candidates when we have a candidate the likes of Obama on the other side are worse than ignorant. They are what Obama's Marxist friends used to call "useful idiots." So, don't pat yourself on the back for your "uncompromising conservatism" as the country we love is dismantled by an Obama presidency working alongside big Demo majorities in the House and Senate. …

Note: Ironically, some of the very same arguments for building a coalition to support McCain were also applicable to supporting Trump, the anti-McCain/establishment candidate in 2016. Meanwhile, "uncompromising conservatism" led to a number of purported conservatives to become NeverTrumpers and de facto Hillary Clinton supporters.

18 October 2008

Day 9/Reason #17: McCain's Energy Policy vs. Obama's Energy Policy

(pictured below)

Photo courtesy of AP.

20 October 2008

Day 11/Reason #15: "Health Care is a Right" vs. a Responsibility Approach

Incredibly, Obama blurted out his true intentions during the second debate on the subject of health care when he told Tom Brokaw that he believes health care is a "right." Almost no American leftists have been brazen enough to state their true views on this subject, but caught off-guard and feeling pretty good about himself, Obama let it go.

On the other hand, McCain advocates a tax-credit approach that would require people to take charge of their own health. There are many personal preferences and choices bound up in health-care decisions. The consequence of allowing the government to control health care would be disastrous.

Obama's approach, coupled with a solid Demo majority, would put us on the road to what Hillary tried to do back in 1992 — government-run health care, or as Joe the Plumber would accurately describe it, "socialized medicine."

If he succeeds in this effort, Obama will have undermined American liberty and our economy in a fundamental way. Our quality of care would diminish, as would our options. Responsibility would diminish. America would diminish.

We must not let this happen.

Note: We did let it happen, however; ironically (but was it surprising?), McCain also incredibly ended the Republicans' efforts to repeal Obamacare in 2017. #thumbsdown

3 November 2008

Day 25/Reason #1: If we are all dead, none of this matters

National Security. It's why I started this blog more than four years ago. Wow, has it been that long?

But national security is the first duty of the federal government. As the Commander in Chief, it's the first duty of the president. Pres. Bush has done an excellent job in protecting America from its enemies since 9/11.

These are serious times ... still. We are at war with Militant Muslims in both Iraq and Afghanistan. Iraq has largely stabilized but the situation in Afghanistan is precarious. Nuclear Pakistan is on the brink, as well, and we are increasingly fighting jihadis there. Iran is trying to develop a nuclear weapon, and it repeatedly threatens Israel with its holocaust-denying madness.

Then there's North Korea and Venezuela. There's growing Russian nationalism and expansionism. There are countries most Americans haven't heard of yet.

If elected, Barack Obama will be tested, all right. Even French President Sarkozy calls Obama's Iran policy "utterly immature."

Foreign policy typically defines presidents, unless they willfully ignore it, a la Clinton. We have enemies now who will not ignore us. The jihadis we are fighting want a fight.

Biden got it right with his recent comments: We tempt our enemies if we elect Obama. Worse yet, we hamstring ourselves. ...

5 November 2008

Congratulations to Barack Obama and the Democrats

Well, we fought hard but came up short. We can discuss what happened and why ... . But that is for another day and time.

Tonight, Barack Obama has defied the odds. Sure, I am disappointed at the outcome, but we must stop for a moment to recognize the magnitude of the achievement.

It started to hit me when I saw Juan Williams choking up describing how amazing the election of America's first black president truly is. Obama himself echoed it. This is a great country. Let there be no doubt that a black man can achieve his dreams in America.

I sincerely hope and pray that I have been wrong about Obama. I don't think I have been, but time will tell. But know this: I am an American first, last and always. Unlike some, I wish the best for our presidents, whether they were/are my choice or not. I won't have Obama Derangement Syndrome. I am a free member of the loyal, conservative ... Republican opposition. I am feeling pretty good tonight, all things considered.

You see, my country has spoken ... and resoundingly. And I am duty-bound to acknowledge and respect what it has said. And I do. Hey, I even know some good people who voted for Obama.

So, tonight, let's pause and recognize the momentous achievement of Barack Obama's election. Let's hope this puts race behind us as a nation ... and for good.

Now, back to work. Saddle up.

McCain doesn't love Bush. He just loves losing to Democrats

… The Economic Meltdown (and McCain's response to it) —The economic meltdown pretty much made McCain's chances of winning slim, unless he had been able to thread the needle with an exceptional campaign. For better or worse, most voters blame the party in power when the economy goes south. And they equate the presidency with "party in power."

To compound this problem, McCain's extraordinarily poor response to the meltdown was really the defining moment of the presidential campaign. First, he suspended his campaign. Then, he went back to Washington and got set up like a stooge by Demos in Congress. Rather than appropriately firing back, McCain pressed for Blessed Bipartisanship. Demos meanwhile stuck knives in his back and prepared to get as many Republicans to sign on to the bailout monstrosity as they could get.

If McCain had listened to me … and Dick Morris, and Rush, and many other conservatives, he would have had a defining issue to campaign on down the stretch. Americans hate the bailout (thank God it has saved us, though … ahem). After all, McCain even could have voted against it and not stopped its passage. He was in a perfect spot. But incredibly he snuggled up next to Obama and voted for the bailout. During this process, too, don't forget that McCain was wildly proposing things left and right on a near-daily basis, i.e., buying back mortgages, firing the SEC Chief, etc.. He railed against corporate greed and excess and couldn't find the heart and energy to go after the Demos who created the Fannie-Freddie mess that was a huge log in the raging economic fire.

Simply put, McCain didn't know what to do, and it showed. Obama just stood there, and he looked like a genius by comparison. Amazingly, McCain singlehandedly put to rest much of the country's doubts about Obama with his own erratic behavior. In such a time, a conservative would have gone back to first principles of the free market.

McCain went back to first principles —bi-partisanship and just doing something, ideas be damned. But elections and politics are about ideas. Election over.

Here's the bottom line: In this toughest of election years, McCain still could have won. The loyal opposition has work to do. But that work is rebuilding a party, and not remaking the country.

Note: This rebuilding effort really started with the defeat of the late Sen. McCain, who, while rightfully respected as a war hero, was a poor standard-bearer for Republicans in general and conservatives in particular. The Republican base's pick of Donald Trump in 2016 was ultimately cemented by the Obama years and Republicans' feckless opposition during that time. The next post shows my attitude in the day-to-day and looking ahead.

1 January 2009

Happy New Year. I Report, but You Decide.

Happy 2009. So, will it be a good year for you and yours ... or not? Perhaps your inclination is to wait to see what circumstances will bring. My retort is that you are a lot more in control of how your year goes than the circumstances you will face.

It appears that a lot of my conservative and Christian brethren are down in the mouth, wondering how we are going to survive these perilous times with the Obama crowd at the helm. I understand their sentiments. This is why I worked to help get the most uninspiring Republican alternative since Bob Dole elected —genuine concern about the alternative.

However, when concern becomes fear and then fear leads to paralysis, well, we do then become subject to our circumstances. We are, in fact, then the subjects of our masters —the unfortunate circumstances that we fear and even loathe.

As for me, I refuse to live in such a way. Rather, I am going to face the Obama years with both dogged determination and a smile. I know that these days will present opportunities for me to shine. The

Carter Malaise spawned the Reagan Revolution, after all. Then, the happy-footed Clinton Administration led to the Contract with America and Republican control of the House for the first time in 40 years.

These sorts of opportunities are about to begin presenting themselves again. Of course, the country (and indeed the world) continues to face the great peril that is Militant Islam. My belief is that we'll see more realism —at least abroad —from the Obama Administration as a result. I think we have already seen a dose of this in his national security picks.

Here's another thing that really keeps me upbeat: My side is right. That is, I really get a charge watching post-modern lemmings charge headlong off reality cliffs. The global warming crowd ... the "we need more taxes" crowd ... the "we can reason with jihadis" crowd ... and the "God is dead" crowd all find that facts are stubborn things when power requires their theories to be tested.

There is a reason why the left uses unelected bureaucracies and judges to push much of its agenda. People want something else; people want what works.

Sometimes I think that insecure conservatives just aren't sure that we are right or perhaps worry what others might think about us when we stand for what is right. As for me, I don't pretend to have the answers to all questions large and small; however, I do believe that I have most of the important stuff right. Thus, I don't fear the post-modern barbarians. They will win some battles here and there, but they'll fold ultimately. I will be there to watch it.

I refuse to waste my time wringing hands and getting down. There is a lot of opportunity in this time. So, let's seize it and make it our time.

Happy New Year.

9 June 2009

I Was Wrong About Obama

It really is that bad …

DC Shutdown: Oh, what the "O" years could have been for this blog. But on his own, Pres. Obama made the case for Trump loud and clear for eight years; and to the extent he failed to make the case, Republicans did their part and chipped in. At least they caused us to pray … Actually, we have been a people of faith long before Obama. Not only were people of faith a key cornerstone of the Trump coalition (with support by evangelicals at all-time levels, for instance), faith in American has been and remains a key component in our national life. My take on this salt and light in our culture is discussed in the next chapter.

Chapter Twelve

Atheists are Scarce in Bomb Craters

13 April 2006
No Corpus Delecti?

Understanding the nature of the celebration, "Happy Easter" is much more politically incorrect than "Merry Christmas."

Christmas announces the arrival of Jesus. Easter proclaims that He actually, physically rose from the dead. Not figuratively. Not a nice ending to a fairy tale. The claim of Easter is one of history. Is it true or not?

The centrality of the resurrection to the Christian message is such that the Apostle Paul wrote in I Corinthians 15 that, without it, "Our preaching is in vain."

So, with all due respect and goodwill to my unbelieving friends, I wish you a Happy Easter. And I hope that the power of the Easter message gives life to your bones.

I won't bore you with all the details, but many moons ago I set out to investigate this claim that Jesus had indeed risen from the dead after the crucifixion. It's easy to believe that He did not. After all, people don't rise from the dead, right?

Here are some of the high points of what I found:

If we start from the premise that an infinite God can do anything, and logically He can, then we must presuppose that anything is possible, including raising Jesus from the dead.

To check the historical record, most of our evidence comes from the Bible. I have found that the Bible was and is reliable historically. Archaeological findings and confirmation by other historical documents continue to confirm this belief. The Bible has more extant manuscripts of any work of antiquity by far. That is, the Bible that we have reliably relates what the authors saw and recorded.

The Bible reports that after Jesus was killed, his ordinary disciples boldly returned to the scene of the crucifixion —Jerusalem — to announce that He had risen. The Bible records that Jesus appeared to more than 500 witnesses. This near-contemporaneous announcement of the resurrection, and at the scene of the crucifixion, is astonishing. Why wasn't such a wild claim immediately put down and refuted?

The mini-revolt by the new Christian sect would have been simple enough to crush, for sure: Simply produce the body of Christ. After all, He was dead, right? But this was never done. And still has not been done. Why not?

But instead of being quickly and easily crushed, the infant faith grew. The 11 disciples fanned out across the known world. Eventually, these men turned the world (including the Roman Empire that condemned Jesus) upside down. All, except the exile John, died martyrs' deaths. So, what happened? When Jesus was crucified, only John did not flee the scene. After the crucifixion, all stayed true to Christ even to the point of death. Yet it wasn't fame, fortune or a televangelism career that motivated them. No, Christ's disciples were ostracized, beaten, jailed, and martyred. Again, for what?

Remember, simply producing the body would have crushed this new movement in its infancy. The most powerful government and military in the world, working with the cooperation of the religious leaders of the day, couldn't produce the body (which it had guarded) and stop all this foolishness? Apparently not.

Instead, the Christian message spread. Christians didn't become extinct. More were added.

The Jewish historian Josephus doesn't mention the resurrection directly. Yet, he understood the significance of the surviving, thriving Christian faith in noting this powerful evidence of the resurrection: "And the tribe of Christians, so named from him, are not extinct at this day."

Perhaps all this uproar was caused by the empty tomb. It was indeed empty, even according to a 6th Century collection of Jewish writings called "Toledot Yeshu."

So, if the tomb was empty, how did it get that way? Again, where is the body? Dead people don't just get up and walk away ... do they?

When the explanations for an event become more fantastic than the event itself, then what do we have?

People can visit the tombs of departed religious leaders, like the Muslims that visit Mohammed's grave. But what about Jesus?

In life, He had no place to lay His head.

Can you truly bury God?

Where is the body?

Happy Easter. ...

23 December 2004
To the Old Scrooge and Back ...

This Christmas Eve I will —per my custom —watch A Christmas Carol, with the fabulous Alistair Sim. This 1951 film is by far the best version of the Charles Dickens' classic, principally due to the brilliant portrayal of Scrooge by Sim. Through Sim's work, we see the various shades of Scrooge ... the shifting emotions, the various twists and sad turns that led Scrooge to his appointment with the spirits on Christmas Eve.

I have always been somewhat of a Scrooge apologist. That is, it perplexes me that Scrooge seems to be remembered almost exclusively for what he was at the beginning of the story —the "old" Scrooge — rather than the man he became at the end of the story. To me, particularly since becoming a Christian myself, Scrooge's repentance and redemption define him. Yet, my view of this great tale continues to evolve even now.

In the last several viewings, I have focused my attention more upon the sad story of Scrooge's life before the fateful Christmas Eve. He was indeed a hated man, so much so that no one would even attend his funeral. His servants would ironically "cast lots" for his belongings. Just how did he get to this point of such intense personal pain that he rejected God and, as a result, his fellow man?

The Road to the "Old" Scrooge

Ebeneezer Scrooge had a relatively happy childhood. His favorite person in the world was his beloved sister Fan. You'll recall that young Ebeneezer started a promising career working for ol' Mr. Fezziwig, the plump, laughing boss known for his great Christmas parties and generosity. As his young career and life progressed, however, Scrooge became more and more like his power-driven colleague and future business partner, Jacob Marley. As Scrooge fell more in love with himself and his own ambition, he then began to lose the love of his fiance Alice. Eventually, as both Scrooge and Alice recognized their paths in life were diverging, the couple broke their engagement.

All of the foregoing might have been bearable for Scrooge, though, if not for the death of his beloved Fan. Scrooge's sister died giving birth to his nephew Fred, that same persistent, annoying lad who kept asking his Uncle Ebeneezer to come to Christmas dinner each year, to no avail, of course. To Scrooge, Fred's invitations were merely reminders of his devastating loss and his aloneness. But who besides Scrooge knew this?

The end of the "old" Scrooge really begins when the Ghost of Christmas Past takes Scrooge back to Fan's death bed to hear words that a young, distraught Ebeneezer never heard: "Take care of my boy." Hearing for the first time Fan's death bed request in light of his long-standing rejection of Fred, Scrooge is heartbroken and sobs ... maybe for the first time ever. Trying to communicate with his long-departed sister, Scrooge cries, "I'm sorry Fan. Please forgive me."

Did Scrooge have even one friend?

Scrooge's life of self-absorption had left him completely alone. His business partner Jacob Marley really was only that —a business partner. It was only after his death that Marley tells Scrooge the hard truth as a friend would: "Mankind was my business!" And in the Cratchit household, even Mrs. Cratchit openly criticizes Scrooge at Christmas dinner, and Bob Cratchit gives Scrooge dutiful loyalty only. The Cratchit family knew of the ugliness that was Ebeneezer Scrooge firsthand. As

Scrooge's dream comes to an end, the Ghost of Christmas Yet to Come points to the bare headstone of Ebeneezer Scrooge. At this point, the truth is evident: Scrooge is on the road to reaping the emotional desolation and desperation that he has sown.

But what of the spirits? Perhaps these are Scrooge's friends. In one sense they are, but in fact they (like Marley) are really just sent upon an errand to visit Scrooge. It would seem then that Scrooge's only friend was the one who sent the spirits to rescue him on Christmas Eve.

Compassion for Scrooge from the One who sent the spirits

The spirits sent to visit Scrooge represent angels sent from heaven, by the Lord Himself. But how can this be, that God would have compassion on this horrible, greedy man who lived alone in a huge house and treated all around him with contempt and disrespect? How truly unlovable a character. God intervened nonetheless.

To me, the redemption of Scrooge illustrates God's unfathomable, amazing grace and unending love. For when all others saw a greedy old man, God saw a man whose bad choices and broken heart had led to spiritual blindness. And in His compassion, God led the spirits to touch the eyes of Scrooge.

But this still doesn't answer the question: "Why?" Why did God show compassion on the sinner Scrooge? Perhaps it was because Scrooge was someone's little boy once, a young man whose foolish choices had taken their toll, and a young man who had lost the most important person in his life. But most importantly, God saw a child of His ... fallen and far away, but no less a child.

That Scrooge's pain and bitterness were largely the result of his own choices was irrelevant. When all the world had given up on him, God was still looking ... still believing.

Compassion of the Son of Man

We Christians often emphasize the deity of Jesus while ignoring His humanity. Thus, while understanding the significance of the deity of Jesus, we miss the complete picture of the Savior. Indeed, Jesus' favorite title for Himself was the Son of Man, a title that emphasizes His humanity. As the Son of Man, He is able to identify with our weaknesses, to understand what it is like to fail, to have broken dreams ... to be alone and without hope. Everyone has a story, and He knows them all. For those alone and hurting at the holidays, He understands and is there.

For some, believing in the God of the Bible is seemingly impossible, for a whole host of reasons. Yet, He understands what it is to be tempted. He understands confronting impossible situations and odds. He sees all, even the ugly that others don't see and that we ourselves don't see, and still He loves us. Indeed, He loves the world. This is mind-boggling yet comforting to me. I think the incomprehensible love and grace of God had a similar effect on John the Apostle, too, for in his Gospel of John he simply called himself "the one that Jesus loved."

Also comforting is that He sees those things in us ... the light, the potential, the unique bent ... that is each person's fingerprint. He seeks out and redeems those qualities for His glory and our good at the same time. Why? I don't know. People can be a lot of trouble and heartache. But I think God does it just because He is good.

The unanswered question

Recall that when Scrooge's worst fears are realized and he contemplates his tombstone and barren grave, he asks the Ghost of Christmas Yet to Come, "Are these things that will be?" Scrooge seeks an answer from this last, appropriately silent and ominous spirit. No answer is given. Anxiety builds. Still no answer ... and then he wakes. Scrooge then realizes that he can help provide the answer. What will he do with the information that he has been given? It is Scrooge's choice, and he makes the right one, of course. As a result, not only Scrooge's life is transformed, but Tiny Tim's and countless other lives are changed and touched in a way that unbelief would not have permitted.

Thus, God saw and pursued the "old" Scrooge when all others had given up and no one else cared or believed in Scrooge. God made a way to get to Scrooge via the three spirits who showed Scrooge his need for redemption. The "new" Scrooge was born, however, only when he dared to believe, to finally trust and allow God into his life.

God bless us, every one. Merry Christmas.

23 November 2005
Happy Thanksgiving ...

... Every morning when you get up, you have at least three things to be thankful for:

1) Your eyes opened. Every day, indeed every breath, is a gift from God;

2) ... [Y]ou are blessed beyond measure and have the opportunity to know God and live this day for Him. Each breath of each day has meaning; and

3) You are an American, and this means that you are among the most blessed people in the history of the world, just by virtue of this fact alone. You have before you the freedom and opportunity to make the most of every breath and every day. So, do it.

No whining allowed. Be thankful. ...

Note: My sons will probably recognize and have heard the foregoing a time ... or two. And in that spirit, the following post was written, as well.

23 November 2006
Happy Thanksgiving: Message to an American Upon Waking

As we celebrate this authentically American and Christian holiday, I am reminded of some reasons for us Americans to be thankful and to Whom we owe thanks. In that spirit, I offer the following encouragement and wish you and yours a Happy Thanksgiving:

Message to an American Upon Waking

If your eyelids opened this morning, thank God.

If you can see, taste, hear, or feel, thank God.

If your eyelids opened this morning and you found yourself in America, thank God.

If you awoke this morning in a foreign land but America is your home, thank God.

If you can go to worship services when and where you choose, thank God.

If you can worship freely and in the quietness of your own soul, thank God.

If you have known someone whose faith made a difference in their life, thank God.

If you have known someone whose faith made a difference in your life, thank God.

If you have ever seen beauty that cannot be adequately described, thank God.

If you have ever experienced a wonder that cannot be fully explained, thank God.

If you can dream, thank God.

If you want to dream again, thank God.

If you can enjoy a good meal today, thank God.

If you have enough money to do at least one thing that brings you joy, thank God.

If you have a job to do, thank God.

If you don't have a job to do but want one, thank God.

If you have a family, thank God.

If you have children, thank God.

If you have a friend, thank God.

If you have someone to spend time with today, thank God.

If your children have driven you mad but you're still not over the edge, thank God.

If you have seen at least one child begin to "get" it, thank God.

If you see your children becoming better than you were and are, thank God.

If you have known someone who caused you to reach for excellence, thank God.

If you have your health, thank God.

If you are sick but long to be well, thank God.

If you have gone through a trial and found yourself stronger on the other side, thank God.

If you have thorns in the flesh but are still pressing on, thank God.

If you have blown it and not gotten what you deserved, thank God.

If you have blown it and gotten what you deserved, thank God.

If you've lived your life such that it's not filled with regret, thank God.

If you've ever needed the chance to start over and got it, thank God.

If you can keep the faith when all around seem to be giving in, thank God.

If you've ever lost faith in yourself but found that someone else still believed in you, thank God.

If you have found joy in living outside yourself, thank God.

If you have been brought joy by others living outside themselves, thank God.

If you are angry and despair over the evil in the world, thank God.

If you have seen sorrow and despair but can still believe and hope, thank God.

If you have found the courage to do what is right when the heat was on, thank God.

If you want to be courageous the next time the heat is on, thank God.

If you can vote, thank God.

If you want to be able to cast a vote, thank God.

If you can comprehend the blessings of liberty such that your life is changed, thank God.

If you have lived in freedom for one day, thank God.

If you have the opportunity to serve America, thank God.

If your way of life has been defended by strangers who volunteered for the privilege of doing so, thank God.

And if you can't think of something for which to thank God, think again.

If you can pray, thank God.

7 April 2007

Easter Saved My Life

… At Easter, I am reminded: One must conquer death to truly live.

Easter is the greatest conclusion to the greatest story ever told. But that's about it for a lot of people. It's a great ending to a great story.

But it's more to me. You see, Easter saved my life.

Whenever I venture directly into matters of faith, I feel the need to send up a flare to remind you again that, though I am most committed to what I am about to say, our friendship is not dependent upon your agreement with me. What is a true friend, anyway? Sounds like a Pontius Pilate moment.

But seriously, I tell you these things from time to time for the same reason that I would tell anyone that I cared about, well, anything.

Indeed, your life may depend on it, as mine did.

When I left for college in 1982, I had the world by the tail. I knew almost all of it, and for that I didn't know, I had the tools to figure it out. My newly-minted Christian faith had a self-righteous and self-assured gleam. (It still shines from time to time, I've been told.)

Well, it seems that some of my professors didn't quite share my appreciation for Christianity. They openly challenged all that I believed. They got to me. I struggled to come to grips with some of their questions, in particular, the intractable question of human suffering. One history professor wondered out loud: "If God is a loving God and in charge of the universe, how could He let 6 million his chosen people die at the hands of a madman?" Good question, I thought then. In fact, I still haven't come up with a good answer.

Others were so skeptical that they caused me to wonder if I could know much of anything. Why not just "bag it" and try wild college girls and the good stuff that this world offered instead? It would have been a lot easier and more fun.

But instead of wild college girls, I wrestled with many questions that I couldn't answer ... like predestination. Oh, man. As I ascended the staircase in my mind, eventually I got to the top. But the questions ... and the understanding of the answers to those questions kept going up, and up ... well-above my mind's staircase.

I wasn't God, and there were things that ultimately I could not know for certain in this life.

But during that fretful, difficult but pivotal year when I was deciding what type of man I would be ... I kept coming back to those things that I could know, at least as well as a human being can know such things.

I came back to the resurrection of Christ. Paul, whose old life as Saul was shattered and whose new life began when he met the risen Christ on the road to Damascus, wrote in I Corinthians 15:14 that, if the resurrection were not true, then his faith would be "in vain."

Wow. Paul, the great rabbi who wrote more than half of the New Testament, staked the whole faith on the resurrection. It seemed pretty straightforward to me. What I really wanted to know was rather what I believed was true. Was Christ really "the Way, the Truth, and the Life?" If he rose from the dead, then He was and He is.

All my other questions were really on the periphery, because if I answered the one question I needed to answer, well, then I could deal with my uncertainties. Mind you, I am not dismissing curiosity or getting answers to serious questions. All I am saying is that answering foundational questions, or rather the foundational question, puts the others in perspective.

I mean, if you knew God was flying the plane you were on, would you worry about the intricacies of the engine?

So, I studied the resurrection. How much? Well, lots have studied it more. But let me put it this way: I've studied it more than anyone I've met who doesn't believe in the resurrection of Christ.

The more you look at truth, the better it looks.

Where is the body, anyway? That's a good starting point. I won't bore you with the details. If you are interested, it's all over the internet. The body of Christ is not, of course. You understand what I am saying.

I concluded that Jesus rose from the dead ... actually, physically rose from the dead. If He was and is God in human flesh, this could be done, after all. And if the resurrection is true, then many things are possible. Death loses its sting, and life has meaning ... every minute of every day.

Believing this, 11 most ordinary and unarmed men turned upside down and conquered the world. In fact, they even went back to the scene of Christ's crucifixion to begin their proclamation of the resurrection.

Eventually, all but one of them would die as martyrs. Only the "disciple that Jesus loved" would not die as a martyr. He was left behind with work to do, you see. In exile, John wrote the Book of Revelation.

Many proofs of the resurrection there are.

But one proof that means so much to me is that ... the truth of Easter saved my life.

DC Shutdown: It seems strange to those who dislike and oppose Pres. Trump that so many people of faith like and support him. I can't speak for everyone, but I do think that many people of faith are tired of claims of righteousness in our leaders and long instead for actions that promote and preserve the place of faith in American life. And Pres. Trump has delivered in this regard, from his judicial appointments to his myriad executive actions in support of life and religious liberty (whitehouse.gov/briefings-statements/president-trump-champion-religious-freedom). From faith, I now turn to the friends who made Daisy Cutter special. The next and final chapter contains some of the best writing in this book, featuring the commenters who made Daisy Cutter go. We had a lot fun along the way, with a fair share of irreverence. We will hit some key issues in the upcoming chapter, too, such as the Demos' disrespect of our electoral process (which continues to the present), the centrality of freedom of speech, and, fundamentally, the need for a positive, persuasive, and bold conservative message to win ... in the era of Trump and beyond.

Chapter Thirteen

Sgt Pepper's Lonely Hearts Club Band

Enjoying the Show and Getting by with a Little Help from my Friends

31 March 2006

"I am an American jurist."

… Just so we are clear, the Boston Herald wants full credit for that marvelous photograph [to the right]. Credit given. And in case you haven't heard about the flap, Justice Antonin Scalia (pictured) made an Italian hand gesture at a nosy Boston Herald reporter/photographer when he was coming out of mass. The reporter went nuts and said that Scalia was flipping him off.

Scalia then wrote a letter to the editor in which he pricelessly asserted that the Herald's reporters are watching too many Sopranos episodes. …

The hapless Herald …gushed how this was a "growing national controversy." [T]he Herald is [offended] that Scalia's gesture was "inside the Cathedral of the Holy Cross." Oh, please. I mean, how did these vampires even get inside there to take the picture ... and in broad daylight?

Really, it sounds like the high school paper staff got a hold of the *Herald's* computers. What's next? No meat loaf on Thursdays? The horrah. The mashed potato lady spit in the gravy? Move her to peas. ...

Unfortunately, more people don't know about this episode. Otherwise, Scalia might get to rock star status. He apparently didn't do "the deed." Frankly, I am disappointed. Can you imagine a picture of Justice Scalia on the front of the *New York Times* flipping off some reporter? He coulda been a contendah.

But some might think he did in fact do it, so he gets credit for doing "the deed." But no "punishment." It's plausible deniability of an act that most normal people would love to do. Great stuff. ...

10 December 2004

Whatever Happened to ...

Ohio Voter Suppression News? These citizens haven't posted in a week. And for that matter, what has happened ... pray tell ... to the recount efforts in general?

Maybe the moonbats have flown to Washington, where the Democrats are engaged in a second recount there ... this one a hand recount.

Maybe Ohio is counting at night, so the moonbats can watch? I don't know. Do they have to hold the card upside down so they can see?

I think the Democrats need to follow through with their pledge and fund this recount effort fully so every vote gets counted. It's about the process, you know, and not about changing the result.

Conspiracy theories die hard, but the Ohio Diebold/missing machine/Rove vote hack-o-tron/massive suppression/there-must-be-a-pony-in-there-somewhere one is going the way of the buffalo with not even a hint of a stampede. What does a bat stampede sound like anyway?

6 January 2005

And ... now this.

Calling all sane people, especially sane Democrats. Even though it is meaningless, I see that some Demos are planning a "contest" to the presidential electors today. …. Apparently, Sen. Kerry is ... trying to have it both ways?

Listen, such things ultimately hurt us all. Endless challenges to elections are becoming the norm, and we will all suffer. For those who think it's only when my guy loses ... I think Washington [Republican] gubernatorial candidate Rossi should give it up, too.

If your currency is valueless, it doesn't matter who holds it. Unfortunately, I think that some behind the endless, baseless challenges to the presidential election know this.

Note: Demos, in their never-ending quest to undermine America's political system, have now contested every presidential election they have lost since 2000. Thanks, Al Gore. But maybe the losses are their candidates' fault?

13 January 2005

Okay ... so, I wrote my pal PW [Charlie, of "Pusillanimous Wanker"]an email to try and diffuse the tension between us

... over my dogmatic Christian worldview [and the prickly comments that had ensued]. To his credit, PW says ... "Call me." So ... I did. A grand conversation ensued. We laughed. He thought I was a "happy" guy. Imagine that. He made some generous comments. Thanks, PW.

Bottom line(s) from our conversation are ... But first, would somebody fire up the Kumbaya, please? There, that's better. Some of you know what a "sucker" I am for Kumbaya.

Okay, here are the punch lines: 1) In spite of our disagreements, I believe PW loves this great land. He has a different vision than I do, and I think his views are dead wrong. He thinks I am a knuckle-dragger;

2) I think PW is wrong about Jesus, and I think his view has serious consequences in this world and the next; 3) I knew I would like PW; 4) He is doing something right, because he has a very pretty wife who seems pretty normal (spends little time blogging, for instance); and 5) the most important thing is ... PW is every bit as precious in God's sight as I am and I want him (and you) to know that this enterprise is not about attacking any one personally.

8 April 2005

Okay, now I am ticked. This thing has eaten two posts. But hey ...

... Man, I must say, the retirements/disappearances in the blogosphere are getting me down. Nickie G. pulled out for the time being. I miss him greatly. ...

Speaking of "retirements," P. Wanker has pulled the plug, too. Man ... where am I going to go to get my retreads of Krugman's insightful columns: "Did you know that GWB actually has the mark of the beast on his scalp?" Dude has some lefty stand-ins over there, but they don't hold a candle. No one can copy a Krugman column like PW and follow it up with something like: "Krugman is righteous. All who disagree are evil ones. Now, go read Krugman's column so you can see what I think and what you must think —or be evil!!!" He is still around and commenting, so maybe he will fly in here and carpet-f-bomb me in the comments. He remains welcome. Open borders. We allow incorrect opinions to immigrate here, so that they can be exposed, corrected, and ultimately used for comedic purposes.

I still like you, PW. XXOOXOXXOO.

18 November 2005

From a pastor friend of mine ... "A Conservative's Parable on Difficulty."

A bird was going to fly south. But he waited too long. When he finally left, his wings froze and he fell to the ground. He lay there dying. Then, a cow came along and crapped on him. This was a terrible experience, but the warm cow crap thawed his frozen wings. He was so happy. He was so happy he couldn't contain himself and he started singing. Then, a cat came along and, to his amazement, wiped all of the cow crap off of him. He was so overjoyed. Alas, but then the cat ate him.

The moral of the story is:

1) Not everyone who craps on you is your enemy;

2) Not everyone who takes crap off you is your friend; and

3) When you are covered in crap, keep your mouth shut.

5 December 2005

Comment Contest ...

Okay, I am using my executive's prerogative to go ahead and merge the finalists and the winner of the Comment of the Year Contest. ...

I will go down the line and recognize some that I just thought were great, all the while working our way to the Comment Champion ...We start with ...

Runners-Up

First, we had Julie, my left-wing friend, who early on saw the way to get ahead in this contest by "poisoning Goomba." Yet, of course, that was before the uber-commenters arrived on the scene. Still, this good-natured dig was great.

I also got a kick out of Pusillanimous Charlie's frustrated cry: "Smile. You're on Terrorist Sympathizer." When the too-serious Charlie got wound up (and ironically let loose), he was pretty good/funny. I also laughed for several days when he called Rhod "Savior Thesaurus." I am giggling now writing about it. Rhod clearly flummoxed the lefty commenters and added a new dimension to this fortified conservative position. Charlie didn't/doesn't seem to appreciate it, and I think that's too bad. The discussion is good, instructive, and usually good for some smiles, as well. They're just words, people, and they're generally not even from people you know. Deep breaths.

Another great comment was provided by Jess, in response to my post regarding the *Newsweek*-created stooge Muslim protesters with signs that looked like Moveon.org had made them. Jess remarked that one of them might have said that his "Naser pin was right under my turbine." Jess quickly gathered himself to point out what I already knew: He meant to say "Nader" pin. But this fumble went into the end zone and was recovered by Jess for a TD. Capturing the protesters' dual mastery of both the English language and the American political system in one sentence was genius. Doing so accidentally was hysterical.

Semi-Finalists

Mark comments often and well, … combining with his fellow Vietnam vet Rhod to create a rhetorical death trap for lefties. Mark has gotten off many good shots, including his dealing the "Air-Dale" card from the bottom of the deck to a McCain supporter and AF vet. … That was pretty good, but … my favorite and funniest, though, was when he got into it with Scott [some lefty commenter from the PW crowd]. Scott pointed out that he, too, served in the military, and Mark remarked: "We used to say there was 99% good troops and 1% shitbird. Were you in the 1%?" This was ROFL material, and I think this was supposed to be a rhetorical question. …

Of course, the Great Goomba had numerous top-notch comments this year. But as a contender for blog of the galaxy, he is ineligible for this little prize. …

The Winner

Rhod. If you have read this blog with any frequency and noted the comments this year, you are aware of the many, many great comments by Rhod. … Great writing. Good humor. Facts. Graciousness. A great guy to have on your side. Sounds like a conservative to me, but hey …

Get a load of some of these great quotes: "Dean is a middle-aged stripper sent to entertain the already-drunk" … the "impacted stupidity of the Left" … leftist angst is like a "pocket of migrating methane."

And Rhod got rolling when the Leftists rolled up on our position here. After one cyber-tantrum, Rhod advised the offending lefty to "busy himself with the mobile above his crib and stop trying to sound like an adult." This is instructive for you aspiring lefty humorists out there. The way to do this humor thing is with subtlety and irony. Stop overreaching. I mean, I know you think I am Satan. But calling conservatives "Satan" is not funny. Talking about you, after a cyber-tantrum, playing with your mobile, is very funny. …

There was this jewel about [then-Sen. Barbara] Boxer's book, which contained horribly written sex scenes, featuring both humans and horses: "The horse sex scene left me feeling happy to be human, and the human sex scenes made me wish I was a horse." …

[Shifting gears and showing his thoughtfulness], there was this poignant comment by the old soldier on the USMC birthday about the passing of a local Marine:

> Last Summer a former Marine up the road from us died suddenly at the age of 69. His name was Norman, but we called him Nobby, for reasons unknown to me.
>
> He ran nearly every day, bicycle-raced, could still do almost 100 pushups, built his own house with a fieldstone tower beside it, rode a Harley, was bright, educated, kind to a fault, and because this is Connecticut, he was our only neighbor with unfailing support for our sons and the Iraq War. He never failed to ask about them.
>
> Even in this foggy liberal swamp, something vanished with Nobby, and it affected everyone for miles around, everyone who knew him. We all thought he'd go on forever, for one thing. But I also believe that everyone felt secure in knowing that such men existed, even the Clintonoids and Kerryites.
>
> Marines are like that. In their excellence they raise the average for us farther than it deserves to go, and the loss of one Marine removes the vicarious courage derived from him by ten other men. Without Nobby the rest of us

have to stand on our own because there's no one
to replace him.

I believe this to be true.

My Three Favorites

The following three winners show the versatility and writing ability of
Rhod.

For instance, in the following comment after [Hurricane]
Katrina, we saw writing that is pretty special:

> The sweep and scope of this terrible thing is to
> be reminded of how complex, and fragile, all of
> our lives are. I look around my realm here and
> see columns and piles of things, but only a few
> which matter. None of them is waterproof or
> permanent but my life would be barren without
> them. I'm blessed to have them, and can do
> without the rest if anyone else needs it.
>
> For countless thousands, even
> something simple like a prescription, or a single
> family photo of an immigrant grandmother,
> down to mortgage documents, a child's band
> instrument or a 3rd grade popstick and yarn
> dream catcher, a favorite book, a family bible, a
> lovely but annoying calico cat or mongrel dog,
> indeed maybe a spouse and all those helpful or
> irritable neighbors, are gone forever. Your life
> swept clean but scuffed, stained and water-
> marked forever in ways visible only to you.
>
> The prattle and incessant yowl of the
> MSM on the agonies and loss are an intrusion
> upon the only way we can understand this
> misery, this churning horror and bottomless
> grief, and that is by making yourself aware of
> what was lost to others by measuring it against

what you have. Then you can really give in the way you're supposed to give, fully aware of your surplus and the hollowness of want a thousand miles away or across the street. I won't do it as long as my hands are full and grabbing for more.

I think, too, that Rhod is really at his best when confronting the Left, like "Anon" who strolled in here and unwisely got off some wild shots before Rhod moved in. The following comment, which typically sent me scrambling for my dictionary, also ties for Comment of the Year:

Anon: Bush raised taxes? Draw and quartering isn't good enough for him. What do you have against tax increases?

Bush defamed McCain? You're lying. This charged was raised by ONE woman at a town hall meeting, proven false by submission of 2000 phone tapes and then broadcast by McCain and Judy Westheimer on NPR. No surprise you seized on it.

Bush's Guard Service and the claims of his CO? C'mon, dope. Even YOU can do better than that.

National Debt. I don't hear any of your Donk Gods complaining about it. It's a two-party problem. This is as worthy a complaint as your others. We're also at war, and one assumes all those national disasters come free of charge. Well, don't they?

I know nothing about Texas politics, but I doubt your figures because you can't keep facts straight anywhere else.

To discuss the progress of the Iraq War with you, or nation building, would be utterly pointless. You wouldn't understand it. What's your alternative, genius? I discount these complaints simply because you have don't have any.

Good God, you're still bleating about the White House vandalism situation? Maybe they were referring to the sink where your God Clinton used to relieve himself, or the blue Gap dress hanger. You better stay away from the subject of Clinton's misdeeds, real or imagined. It's quicksand for you.

Tax cuts for the wealthy? This saw is so old it doesn't even cut through the jellyfish spine of a Democrat.

Your last two paragraphs are so utterly without merit and hysterical that I won't address them.

Keep that asafetida bag around your neck full of lavender and garlic. That way Bush won't get you.

So, with all of its fact-based argumentation and vivid descriptions, the two previous comments tie with, yes tie, with yet another ... for Comment of the Year. That would be Rhod's reference to Ted Kennedy as the Demo Party's "rotten sea bass on the pier. The stench and sight of the thing is horrific, but no one wants to pick it up and carry it off. Thus, they hope that the birds will take it away." I think I smelled the thing through the keyboard. Humor but with a biting, dead-on point.

So there you have it. Prizes? Well ... I think Goomba is going to split his Weblog Award winnings or something like that. No? Maybe I will send Rhod a free shirt if I ever make them. Don't know. In the meantime, a free subscription to this website for the next year, Rhod.

So, congrats to Rhod and many thanks. And thanks to you all for making this a much better space by your input.

Note: Rhod was most certainly the best writer to post at Daisy Cutter.

2 August 2006

No "Cabins," no "Chats," no "Pizza" ... Jihadis aren't kidding, but we're laughing

Saw an incredible story over the weekend and was expecting much more blog buzz about it. But that's okay. Here, we'll call it "developing" ...

It seems that Iran's mini-mullah in a sportcoat, Mahmoud Ahmadinejad, has decreed foreign words off-limits, including the insidious "pizza." Yes, it's true. In Iran, pizza shall hereafter only be lawfully be referred to as "elastic loaves."

... There's more. Hang on.

The Associated Press also reported that "a 'chat' will become a 'short talk' and a 'cabin' will be renamed a 'small room.'"

Thus, gay Republicans will now be referred to as "Small-Room-Made-of-Logs Zionist-Fascists."

Indeed, language is powerful, even transforming. But so is humor. There are very few things as funny as someone who is not trying to be funny but is very funny but doesn't understand how funny he is. This is very funny indeed.

Don't misunderstand. I fully understand the evil that Ahmadinejad and his ilk represent. But I also understand that almost all thinking people know the value of a good laugh.

English essayist William Hazlitt said that people with a sense of humor understand the difference between the way the world is and the way that it ought to be. I've always liked that thought very much.

I would like to take this thought even farther and posit the following: You need a sense of humor as a nation to maintain your influence and preserve your place in the world.

America, of course, is the land of the free, the brave, and the funny, as all the world knows. And witness the Brits ... the land of Mr. Bean and Monty Python. As for Israel, well, you need a sense of humor to have the Muslim world surrounded for nearly 60 years.

Canada? There's lots of funny people there, but there are limits to this hypothesis.

Now, back to Ahmadinejad, just look at him. Look at the whole lot of the jihadis while you're at it.

No humor. No sense of proportion. Elastic loaves? Are you kidding me? How can he not know how hilarious that is to be spending time, effort and energy worrying about "pizza," "cabins" and other deleterious phrases?

Surely the bulk of the Iranian population laughs privately.

But their leaders don't understand difference between the way the world is and the way it ought to be.

So, we who do will laugh.

And keep on surviving.

Note: An underrated trait of Pres. Trump is his sense of humor, too.

15 January 2007

A moderate is right at least once in his life?

Witness Pres. Gerald Ford. I read over the weekend that in interviews with his local paper Ford said that Pres. Reagan got too much credit for ending the Cold War. Actually, Ford deserves the credit, it turns out ... because of the Helsinki Accords. Oh, my. Those Helsinki Accords broke the Soviets' backs, all right.

Like I said, until this weekend, I had no evidence that a moderate had ever been right, unless political circumstances force him/her to behave as a conservative.

Then I read that Ford said that Carter was a "disaster" who was the "worst president of my lifetime."

Eureka.

Of course, in true moderate fashion, Ford's comments were not permitted to be released until he was literally out of Dodge.

So, Ford's beautiful, 3-point off-the-glass shot of truth against Carter is hereby ruled disqualified, as it was launched "after the buzzer," so to speak.

They [moderates] are still worse than stopped clocks.

Pres. Ford shook my worldview to its core, but the rule still stands: No living moderate has ever said anything of substance that is true.*

Disclaimer: *Unless posing as a conservative for political reasons.

2 July 2007

Last time I'm ever doing one of these things ...

... Julie: In college I learned how to shoe a horse and scale the brick wall of the men's dorm.

DC: Most exciting thing I have scaled is probably the Confidence Course at Quantico, with a nice, thin layer of ice on it.

Julie: I come from a family of writers. (sadly that doesn't help out this blog)

DC: I come from a family of blue collar people. Neither of my parents finished college. My dad was a traveling salesman for most of his days, until the rise of Wal-Mart. My mother was a bookkeeper and worked for many years managing gas stations for Mobil Oil. She was held up a couple of times and kept on doing it. A couple of guys tried to hold up my dad once, but he had his bat with him (I come from a family of baseball fans, too.) My mother wanted me to become a lawyer. My dad never forgave me for becoming one.

19 May 2006

Farewell Nickie: Remembering my Blog Brother [the Weblog Award-Winning "Nickie Goomba"]

Nickie and me ... I came to know "Nickie Goomba" through his and my association with Homespun Blogger. When I signed up, I took a spin through the various blogs on the Homespun blogroll. Trying to get my fledgling blog off the ground, I paid visits and tried to comment where I could. A few bloggers reciprocated. Nick came by. At the time, he called his blog "Hey relax ... I was just sayin.'" I thought that was a funny, catchy title.

I returned to his blog and began to notice that he was genuinely funny and creative. I mean he was really funny, often irreverent. He was also a real-deal conservative. He was a giving soul and was constantly promoting others' blogs, too.

As I got exposed to the blogging world, I noticed that a lot of bloggers visit blogs and comment, hoping that others would return to their blog. This is certainly fine, and I did some of this. Funny, at first I visited Nick's blog hoping to get him to come back to mine. Soon, I found that I wanted to go there just to see what he was saying.

We became fast friends during the '04 election cycle. We both worked our respective spheres of influence, he in Northern California and me in Texas. He was very supportive of this blog. We worked hard for Pres. Bush.

We got hacked together, although mine was minor hit. Nick's was a major job. In fact, I think he got hit twice. I remember rolling up on his site, and it looked like he had changed the language setting to Russian or maybe Farsi. Oh, man. It was bad. I emailed him and his response was ... "They got me good." I could almost hear him panting, but smiling, too. He promised to be back soon.

He was. When he returned, the blog was simply called "Nickie Goomba." The Italian self-deprecation and no-PC-zone commentary was priceless. The comedy was taken to a new level. Armed with photoshop, he was a force.

Of course, he created the blogopshere's crack news service, that is, the "Goomba News Network." Via GNN, Nick would chronicle the latest developments in the world through the eyes of his staff of "reporters." Of course, the craziness chronicled was sometimes hard to separate from fiction, or was it truth? And if you watched and read closely, you could tell you were dealing with a comedic genius. A good example of this was his semi-haphazard usage of bold type. It was subtle, yet roaring hilarity, humor at the highest level.

All the while he was communicating a point ... He loved his country and his fellow man. He wouldn't give up his fight for conservative principles or the nation. And he wouldn't sacrifice people in the process. He was unique.

When someone gets you laughing over something rather serious, walls are torn down and bridges are being built. When bridges are built, then people ... and ideas ... can move.

This was the business of Nickie Goomba.

And while blogging away at his first-rate site, he ... kept in touch and was a generous commenter, here and elsewhere. His comments were funny and generally pithy. He occasionally was serious, and when this happened we caught a glimpse of his super-sized heart. He was particularly moved by last year's Memorial Day Address [reprinted in Chapter 7], as it brought back memories of his own service and that of his friends who did not return from Vietnam. ... I remember his writing that "I am crying now, as I write this." ...

In spite of his work in real life, he was generous with his time, and he helped many of us out with either design or other questions. He introduced me to his Italian blogger friends and helped me to learn to love and appreciate Italy more. He showed me the way to great international blogs like Free Thoughts and Big Pharaoh. And, by the way, Nick designed the logos for both. He was a fantastic talent.

And this fantastic talent was an ally of freedom-seeking and freedom-loving people everywhere.

Goomba did a button for me once, too, just trying to be helpful and supportive. And ... I wrote him an email with a blogging question once and asked him to give me a call on my cell phone. Less than an hour later, the phone rang. It was Goomba.

We had a great talk. He had a beautiful New York accent. He answered my question and put me at ease. ... He asked me what I did, and I told him I was a lawyer. "We've got to get you into politics," he gushed. I told him that just goes to show that even the great Goomba has poor judgment sometimes. "That's just what we need ... another lawyer in politics," I said. He thought that was a good point: "Never mind." We laughed. ...

From my brain ...

What we can learn from Nickie's blogging career is that quality matters. I went to his blog first for traffic but returned because of the quality that was there ... and on a consistent basis.

Many in the blogging world use their forums to rant and launch screeds into cyber-nowhere. Then, they in turn want others to come and read same. Well, we each have our various spheres of influence. For instance, I know a loyal cadre in my neck of the woods who will come by and read what I have to say. ...

But we can't demand readers. To expand our reach and influence, we need to produce quality content. We need to do something that others aren't doing, or we need to do what others are doing but better. Nickie did both. Thus, he had a real impact.

He did it with humor, a positive tone, and by not taking himself too seriously. Boy, can we learn a lot from his example now?

Positive stuff works, and I am not talking Pollyanna, either. People want to laugh, to be inspired, to believe. People want solutions and a way to go. There's a lot to believe in, still. Nick knew that.

From my heart ...

If you search "Goomba" at this blog, you'll find quite a few references. Nick cut a wide swath here. He both inspired content and made existing content better. He always asked the first question at our "pressers," and the back and forth with him helped me and this blog. A lot. ...

And his spirit won't let me believe that such a spirit won't continue to grow and flourish in America.

He cared about people. He cared about ideas, but not at the expense of people. We can learn from this. He was a gracious host at his blog, and he welcomed differing views. He was about advancing ideas, not shuffling past or climbing over nameless faces in a crowd.

Here was his last post:

> It is with great sadness that I close down the
> blog. Keep fighting the fight against the Left's

insanity. When God gives me the opportunity to reappear, I'll be angrier and sillier than ever. I shall return.

> Nickie Goomba

… So, in remembering Nickie, maybe we ought to take some time today or this weekend to remember that life is fleeting. Be good to those in your life and sphere of influence. Live outside yourself. Find your life by giving it away. If you need to say something to make a relationship right or better, do it today. Serve God and your country. Live while you can.

Nickie Goomba did.

So, here's to you, Nickie.

Here's to the greatest blogger I ever knew. …

Afterword

Here's a note I received from Julie that sounds a somewhat familiar refrain:

> … Nickie … was a wonderful supporter when I started the blog. I had asked him long questions about how he learned to write and what inspired him (besides all of us wussy liberals) and he always wrote back with care and interest. Odd how you can miss so much someone that you never really "knew." I'm sure you feel this more keenly as you and Nickie had a close and hilarious camaraderie. …

And thanks to the great post/synopsis at *American Daughter* for pointing me back to the final exchange with Nickie here at Daisy Cutter. … I thought it appropriate to end this tribute with our final exchange:

> Coulter has been stealing your stuff for years.
> Nickie Goomba 04.25.06—5:06 am

> Nick,

Is that you? Hold on while I kiss the computer screen. There.

DC 04.25.06—6:11 pm

My health is improving. Am in a remote Italian village getting healthy again. I am walking almost 15 minutes per day and I will soon be sprinting. Count on me blogging again by June. … Maria snarls hello.

My very best to you, Mark & Rhod. DC, your kind words and sentiments have meant so much to me. I cannot wait to get back.

At the moment, I am on the keyboard of a young man who has one of the few internet computers in this village. He is suspicious of my slow typing and careful structuring of sentences. If I dare to complain of his glare, the polizia will certainly be called to this location, post haste.

Truly, my love and respect to you all.

Nickie Goomba 04.27.06—9:25 am

Note: Rich DiGiorgis, the self-styled "Nickie Goomba," fulfilled his dream of becoming an Episcopal priest after his blogging days were over. He walked with me through some of the toughest days of my life, and he officiated over one of the very happiest—when I married my amazing wife Jodi on January 15, 2016. A little more than a year later, Rich passed away after a long and valiant battle with cancer.  I still cherish our friendship and am grateful for how he made Daisy Cutter—and me—better. See you on the other side in the Celestial City, my brother.

Epilogue

Final Post

4 July 2010
Independence

A little over six years ago ... that's been a while ... I started blogging in this space. A lot has changed on a personal level (and beyond, for sure) since then. It's been fun. ...

But I will still be around the internets from time to time. ...

Who knows? I may be back at some point in the future here, but for now, I can't see such a time. So, I am going to leave this site here as a museum of sorts of ideas and of one solitary Christian conservative speaking out on behalf of what he believed ... and believes ... during a most tumultuous and important time in our history. Maybe my kids will read it someday. For those of you who know them and feel led to direct them here, I would appreciate it.

One thing I believe in ... is America. I love my country so, to me, it's more like a love story and a relationship with the land I live in. I realize that for many (even those who agree with me on a lot of things), this might seem a bit much.

But I was taught to love my country ... because it is good, decent, and free. And the brave have inhabited this place since its founding. I stand on their shoulders ...

No particular government nor politician can dampen this for me.

Note: Who knows? Maybe I will turn this blog into a book once I see how the issues, ideas and themes discussed herein ultimately led us to the election of Donald Trump and the ongoing shake-up of our political system. It's been a much-needed development, indeed, and I look forward to continuing to lend my voice and efforts to it in service to the nation.

Our most precious resource is time, and I thank you for investing yours to read this book. If something here has caused you to think, or even better, to do something about those thoughts to make this nation a better place for all Americans, well, great.

If you have comments or questions, please email me at rickrutline@gmail.com or visit me on the web at www.dcspeaks.net.

Semper Fidelis,
Rick Rutledge
aka "DC"